Civic Engagement Across the Curriculum

A RESOURCE BOOK FOR SERVICE-LEARNING
FACULTY IN ALL DISCIPLINES

Civic Engagement Across the Curriculum

A RESOURCE BOOK FOR SERVICE-LEARNING
FACULTY IN ALL DISCIPLINES

Richard M. Battistoni, Ph.D.

Campus Compact

THE PEW CHARITABLE TRUSTS

The Mission of Campus Compact

Campus Compact is a national coalition of college and university presidents committed to the civic purposes of higher education. To support this civic mission, Campus Compact promotes community service that develops students' citizenship skills and values, encourages collaborative partnerships between campuses and communities, and assists faculty who seek to integrate public and community engagement into their teaching and research.

This publication has been made possible with support from the Ewing Marion Kauffman Foundation and The Pew Charitable Trusts.

Campus Compact
Brown University
Box 1975
Providence, RI 02912
phone: (401) 867-3950
email: campus@compact.org
website: www.compact.org

ISBN: 0-9667371-8-0

Table of Contents

Assignments & Exercises Contained in the Appendix   iii

Preface   v

The Rationale: Evidence of a Crisis in Democratic Civic Education   1

Civic Engagement Across the Curriculum   9

What Is Good Citizenship? Conceptual Frameworks in the Social Sciences   13

What Is Good Citizenship? Conceptual Contributions from Other Disciplines   19

Beyond Conceptual Frameworks: The Practical Skills of Engaged Citizenship   31

What Is Good Citizenship? Student Voices   41

Being Attentive to the Civic Dimensions of Service-Learning   51

References   57

Appendix   69

List of Assignments and Exercises
CONTAINED IN THE APPENDIX

Appendix A: How Do You Define Citizenship?   71

Appendix B: Reflection Questions That Tap Civic Dimensions   72

Appendix C: Public Problem Statement and Organizational Issue Research   73

Appendix D: Philosophy of Service Assignment   74

Appendix E: Semester Project—Drama and Public Value   75

Appendix F: Action Plans Assignment   76

Appendix G: Coalition Building Exercise   78

Appendix H: Organizational Action Research Assignment   79

Appendix I: Final Service Site Team Presentation Assignment   81

Appendix J: Curricular Revision Exercise   82

Appendix K: Rhetoric and Public Opinion Paper Assignment   84

Preface

Over the course of this semester I have become a citizen of New Brunswick. It could be argued that I was a citizen here well before registering for the course, but I did not feel as if I were one. Having taken the course, I now know why I felt as I did. A citizen must play an active role in his or her community. A citizen must work for change, and never accept the status quo—things can always be better. I am now aware of what is happening around me....I now see the city differently. I'm no longer scared walking to [my service site]—far from it. I feel like I know that small portion of the city now. Now when I pass people on the street, some say hello to me, and call me by name. Through my work I've gotten to know individual people, and they've gotten to know me. I enjoy my community service. It has opened my eyes as to the role I play as a citizen in my community.

These words come from Daniel Terner, a student who took one of my introductory service-learning courses at Rutgers University in the Fall of 1993. The words were taken—with Daniel's express permission—from a writing assignment in the course, asking students to make a connection between their community service in the class and their identity as citizens in a democracy. It exemplifies the hope of many in higher education (and K-12 education, for that matter) that service-learning programs can cause students to come away with a better and more critical understanding of their communities and their own roles as citizens in them.

This hope is fully expressed in the recent Campus Compact *Presidents' Declaration on the Civic Responsibility of Higher Education,* now endorsed by more than 400 college and university presidents (Campus Compact, 1999). In this document, campus leaders commit themselves "to renew our role as agents of our democracy, [to] catalyze and lead a national movement to reinvigorate the public purposes and civic mission of higher education" (Campus Compact, 1999: 3–4). Actually, the Presidents' Declaration reflects a major change in the way campuses are viewing their civic mission, and the role of service in this mission. In a little over a decade, the ultimate aim has shifted from promoting community service to institutionalizing service-learning, and now to fostering student civic engagement in a diverse democracy.

Why the shift to civic engagement? And why is civic engagement a concern for faculty in all disciplines? The contemporary concern about citizen apathy runs very deep, and campuses are searching for ways to combat civic disengagement through the use of service-learning. This resource book attempts to provide the rationale for action across the curriculum, along with the conceptual and practical tools all interested faculty will need to accomplish the goal of linking their service-learning efforts to civic engagement outcomes.

Throughout this volume faculty will be presented with different ways of thinking about civic engagement, ones which may be more relevant to their own disciplines than more traditional conceptions of citizenship. The volume also contains valuable practical resources for moving students from service to civic engagement, including sample course assignments, exercises, and reflection questions. These resources are listed on page iii, and can be found in the appendix at the back of the book.

chapter one

The Rationale:
EVIDENCE OF A CRISIS IN DEMOCRATIC CIVIC EDUCATION

Too many of us have become passive and disengaged. Too many of us lack confidence in our capacity to make basic moral and civic judgments, to join with our neighbors to do the work of community, to make a difference. Never have we had so many opportunities for participation, yet rarely have we felt so powerless. In a time that cries out for civic action, we are in danger of becoming a nation of spectators.

—National Commission on Civic Renewal, 1998

While campus support for service-learning has, from the beginning, been connected to a concern about a "crisis" in American civic education, the concern has grown over the past two decades. With mounting evidence of disengagement, especially among young people, from American politics and public life, there is an ever deepening feeling that our educational institutions are leaving students unprepared for a life of engaged, democratic citizenship.

The concern about civic apathy and disengagement begins with voting. As we all know, the seemingly most basic and easy civic responsibility, voting, is on a 40-year decline in the U.S. As late as 1960, almost two-thirds of the eligible electorate cast their ballots in presidential elections. But beginning in 1972, the rate of those voting plummeted until not even half of the eligible electorate bothered to show up in 1996. A small blip upward took place in 2000, not very impressive considering the massive efforts and amounts of money that were expended to register and turn out voters across the nation. In off-year elections the numbers are even lower; a little over one-third voted in 1998. Young people between the ages of 18 and 24 have consistently participated at a rate below that of those above the age of 25. In 1996, fewer than one-third of eligible 18- to 24-year-olds voted. And in 1998, it is estimated that only 18 percent of those under 25—and only 11 percent of 18- to 19-year-olds—voted. In a survey of 15- to 24-year-olds commissioned by the National Association of Secretaries of State (NASS) two years ago, only 12 percent of those 15 to 24 years old agreed with the statement that voting is a basic tenet of good citizenship (Tarrance Group and Lake, Snell, & Perry, 1999). Benjamin Barber once stated, "In a country where voting is the primary expression of citizenship, the refusal to vote signals the bankruptcy of democracy" (Barber, 1998).

The concern about youth civic disengagement goes well beyond voting, however. A number of studies conducted over the past several years—including the report from the National Commission on Civic Renewal cited at the beginning of this section—state in unmistakable language the extent to which traditional college-aged citizens are turned off from politics and public life. In a study conducted for the Kettering Foundation, *College Students Talk Politics,* focus groups of college students indicated extreme political alienation and pessimism, many concluding that "politics has nothing to do with my life" (Harwood Group, 1993: v). The report of the annual "Freshman Survey" from the Higher Education Research Institute (HERI) in the fall of 2000 showed political engagement at an all-time low in the history of the survey, even though it was an election year where "freshman interest in politics traditionally increases" (Sax, et al., 2000; for summary results from 2000 survey, see: www.gseis.ucla.edu/ heri/news.htm). A poll of college students conducted in January 2000 by the Mellman Group for the Panetta Institute echoed these bleak findings about youth political disengagement. One of the students interviewed for this survey said that "there is such a negative connotation to politicians and the whole field of politics that it doesn't interest me to get involved in such a hypocritical situation" (Panetta Institute, 2000). A number of studies indicate that youth pay little attention to news reporting on public affairs (see Bennett, 2000, for a complete account of youth political apathy and avoidance of news media).

Well, you might say, this is a function of youth turnoff from politics as it is traditionally understood, and given all that goes on in politics that gets reported, it is no wonder that they are turned off. They have every reason to be disillusioned with partisan politics, political incivility, and their own seeming political impotence, inherited from our and previous generations. So maybe we need to look at some other indicators of civic or public engagement, things young people have opted into as alternatives to traditionally understood political engagement. But if we look at the kinds of things that commentators going all the way back to Alexis deTocqueville saw as indicators of civic participation and vibrant public life (voluntary associations in civil society, social capital, even "community identity"), we see similar disengagement there as well. Young people seem to be "joining" less and identifying less with matters indicative of public engagement. In responses to surveys, they say that they do not want to be actively involved in the community, they don't see themselves as future community leaders, nor do they want "to make the community a better place to live" (all socially desirable answers, by the way, making the findings more remarkable—see Putnam, 2000; Panetta Institute, 2000).

On a more personal note, a conversation I had during the spring semester 2000 with students in a course on democratic theory and practice seems to confirm this disillusionment. At the beginning of the course, I ask students to bring an artifact—news story, advertisement, movie/video selection, piece of music, etc.—that they think demonstrates U.S. popular culture's view of democracy. As they had in the past, students in the spring 2000 course brought in the usual array of items—two songs by R.E.M., one by Bob Dylan, excerpts from commercial films such as *Independence Day* and *A Few Good Men,* images from the webpage of Ben & Jerry's and the internet-based company Ameritrade—but one presentation, and the discussion that followed, was particularly telling. One student chose the MTV show "Total Request Live," where viewers can log onto a website and vote from a large list of posted songs for the music video they want to see. The show plays the top ten vote-getting videos, counting down to number one. The student, in presenting orally and in written comments following, said, "I believe that this system is extremely democratic because it allows the people to see what they want to watch on TV and express what they feel about it. It is one of the great opportunities for common people to actually voice their opinion and see results, more than what they see in a real democratic setting most of the time." When I pressed this student and the rest of the class to think about whether this was an example of democratic consumption or democratic citizenship (I think I actually asked whether decisions about the music video that I get to watch was in the same realm as the health care I want my government to guarantee, or the person who will represent me in the legislature), the entire class supported this example of democracy, because it was an example of a case where a person's input mattered, where people had the opportunity to request change and actually see the change take place before their eyes. This was a contrast to what they saw in politics.

I choose this story not to bash students, but to suggest that students, especially those of immediate post-secondary age, come to our campuses with few experiences of lived democracy—let alone respect for their autonomy or voice—either in their schools or in their daily lives outside of school. With all of the new experiments in teaching and learning, we can still question, as John Dewey did more than 80 years ago: "Why is it, in spite of the fact that teaching by pouring in, learning by a passive absorption, are universally condemned, that they are still entrenched in practice?" (Dewey, 1916:38). With few exceptions (see Meier, 1995), students complete secondary education in an environment that is dominated by knowledge transmission and recall, where the product (a grade, a high test score, a diploma) always seems to trump the learning process. The process and its outcomes are dictated by those adults who are in charge, not by the students in collaboration with their teachers or educational policymakers.

Moreover, the educational systems within which they learn more often ask students to be consumers rather than producers of knowledge (for a political critique of this understanding of students-as-consumers, see Boyte & Kari, 2000; for an epistemological critique, see Liu, 1995).

Higher Education's Response to the Crisis

> We challenge you to assure that the next year's entering students will graduate as individuals of character more sensitive to the needs of community, more competent to contribute to society, and more civil in habits of thought, speech, and action.
>
> —Wingspread Group Report on Higher Education, 1993

Educators have taken note of this growing trend toward youth civic disengagement. Higher education, in particular, seems concerned about the growing crisis and is sensitive about its own failings in engaging students as active citizens in their democracy. The Kettering *College Students Talk Politics* report charged that higher education "appears to leave students without concepts or language to explore what is political about their lives" (Harwood Group, 1993: xii). When the National Commission on Civic Renewal reported on the state of civic disengagement in 1998, it seemed to offer no role for higher education in providing solutions. Once again, academia was subjected to the charge of being irrelevant to public problems, unresponsive to public needs; in the words of Derek Bok, "Communities have problems, universities have departments" (Bok, 1990). Campus Compact's recent efforts, as exemplified in the Presidents' Declaration, can be seen as a response to this charge of civic deficiency on the part of higher education. So, too, are the calls of prominent scholars—such as Lee Benson & Ira Harkavy (1997), Ernest Boyer (1994; 1996), Benjamin Barber (1992), and Derek Bok (1990)—for American colleges and universities to return to their earliest mission of educating citizens for democracy and liberty.

The most common initial strategy for meeting the challenge of stemming the tide of civic disengagement, particularly favored by college and university presidents, has been to adopt programs placing students in community-based service activities. In fact, my initial service-learning activities were inspired by a university president, Edward Bloustein of Rutgers, The State University of New Jersey, whose 1988 graduation address was a call to action. President Bloustein issued a challenge to the graduates and to the entire university community, to combat what he saw as the twin "pathologies"— he called them "shibboleths"—of the 1980s: 1) the persistence of "racism, sexism, homophobia, religious intolerance, and fear of and animosity toward 'foreigners;'" and 2) an excessive individualism and lack of civic engagement. He saw these two problems as interconnected, for he strongly believed that by moving beyond ourselves and encountering others in community that we could come to an appreciation of the strength and great capacities contained in the diverse assemblage of people that make up the U.S. (and at the time, New Jersey and Rutgers mirrored this great diversity). At the end of this challenging address, he called for integrating community service as a requirement for graduation, as both a solution to his two concerns, and as a valued ingredient in all liberal education (Bloustein, 1999). Inspired by the vision contained in this address, I began to get involved in using what has come to be called service-learning as a pedagogy with the ultimate learning aim of education for effective participation in a diverse, democratic society.

At the time, Ed Bloustein was a pioneer, but he certainly was not alone among leaders in higher education. In 1985, a group of college and university presidents formed Campus Compact with the explicit goal of raising the civic concern of their students through campus-based community service programs. A year earlier, the formation of a new student run organization, the Campus Outreach Opportunity League (COOL), also helped spur new community service initiatives on the nation's campuses. Neither Campus Compact nor COOL in these initial stages was oriented toward classroom based *service-learning* programs; but, by the end of the decade, largely through the efforts of the National Society for Experiential Education, many educators began to link experiential pedagogy to the burgeoning student community service movement. From a 1989 Wingspread conference report sponsored by the Johnson Foundation and through a three-volume NSEE publication *Combining Service and Learning* (NSEE, 1990), awareness of service-learning both as a pedagogy and a means of civic education began to spread through both the higher education and K-12 educational communities. By 1992, the federal government's Learn and Serve America program began to provide funding resources for service-learning initiatives in higher education, and in 1993 the Corporation for National Service's definition of service-learning was revised to include the goal of "foster[ing] civic responsibility." By the latter half of the 1990s, not only Campus Compact but also the Association of American Colleges and Universities, the American Association for Higher Education, the American Council on Education, the Council of Independent Colleges, the National Association of State

Universities and Land Grant Colleges, and most of the other higher education organizations had endorsed community-based learning as one component in education for engagement in democracy.

Can Service-Learning Be a Vehicle to Civic Engagement?

The idea behind all of these efforts has been to capitalize on the heightened involvement by youth in community service to advance the mission of civic engagement. Here, the evidence clearly shows volunteering on the rise, especially among young people. Against the numerous indicators of youth civic disengagement, Robert Putnam reports that the propensity to engage in community service is the single form of civic involvement in which young people under 30 years of age are more engaged than their immediate elders, and the trend seems to be on the rise among even younger children (Putnam, 2000: 130, 133). The experience of young people entering college in 1999, as reported in the annual Higher Education Research Institute (HERI) Freshman Survey, confirms this finding with a record high 75.3 percent reporting having volunteered in the year prior to attending college (Sax, et al., 2000).

Of course, this strategy assumes a clear relationship between service and citizenship. Does this relationship exist? Can service-learning be seen as a vehicle for enhancing civic engagement in a diverse democracy? Some research suggests that this increase in one-on-one community service seems not to have had the broader impact on civic engagement that proponents of service-learning desire. Putnam reports that while individual volunteering has gone up, other important indicators of youth civic engagement, such as active participation with others in community groups, has declined (Putnam, 2000: 130). It may be that students are consciously choosing community service over political engagement, volunteering as an antidote to the venom of political life. Recent data from the HERI Freshman Survey, the National Association of Secretaries of State, the Panetta Institute, and the Harvard University Institute of Politics all suggest that while more young people are volunteering, fewer are seeing any connection between service and political engagement, which continues to rank low in importance in their lives (Sax, et al., 1999, 2000; Tarrance Group and Lake, Snell, & Perry, 1999; Panetta Institute, 2000; Institute of Politics, 2000). At the very least, we would expect that the more than 12,000 service-learning courses that Campus Compact tells us exist on college campuses should be having a countervailing positive civic effect. Instead, we continue to hear anecdotal reports from faculty and other educators that community service not only fails to connect students to public life, but it may tend to reinforce student stereotypes about people who are "different" from the community being served, hardening previously held views. Harry Boyte has concluded that, when done inadequately, "community service is not a cure for young people's political apathy" because "it teaches little about the arts of participation in public life" (Boyte, 1991: 765).

On the other hand, evidence does exist to confirm the assumptions of college and university leaders like Ed Bloustein of Rutgers, that service-learning has a positive impact on civic engagement. Of course, I have often made this claim that citizenship education can be a powerful foundation and outcome for service-learning, based on my experiences teaching courses on three different urban campuses. My students' own reflections—as evidenced in the excerpt at the beginning of the preface and those scattered throughout this book—indicate that a community service experience connected to courses centered on education for democratic citizenship can achieve the goal of educating young people about their responsibilities in a democratic society, allowing them to think about what it means to be a part of the multiple communities in which they find themselves (for a more extensive treatment, see Battistoni 1997a).

But beyond my own experiences, a greater body of evidence confirms that when accompanied by proper preparation and adequate academic reflection, service-learning can be a potent civic educator (see, for example, Farr, 1997; Guarasci, 1997; Markus, et al., 1993; Mendel-Reyes, 1997; Rimmerman, 1997a; Eyler & Giles, 2000; Walker, 2000; Cammarano, Battistoni, & Hudson, 2000). The best study— from a scientific perspective—remains the frequently cited Markus, Howard, and King (1993) study of students in a political science class at the University of Michigan. Those students randomly assigned to the two of eight discussion sections with a service component showed greater change than the other students in the course in the following areas: their intention to serve others, their like- lihood to give to charity, their orientation to others, their sense of social responsibility, their belief that one can make a difference, and their tolerance. A "Measuring Citizenship Project" study conduct- ed by Rutgers University's Walt Whitman Center for the Culture and Politics of Democracy indicated that students enrolled in citizenship-based service-learning courses at Rutgers had a stronger sense of civic capacity and membership than students enrolled in two different comparison courses, and scored higher on a "diversity and tolerance" scale developed by the project. On a "civic leadership" scale of the Measuring Citizenship survey—a scale consisting of 23 items that ask respondents to compare themselves with others with regard to a variety of civic leadership skills and capacities— Rutgers service-learners scored significantly higher from pre- to post-test than those in non-service- learning political science and journalism classes (Walt Whitman Center, 1996).

Evaluations of college programs supported through the Corporation for National Service's Learn and Serve America Higher Education Program have produced overall positive findings in regards to pro- motion of civic responsibility (Sax and Astin, 1997; Gray, Ondaatje, and Zakaras, 1999). A 1996 sur- vey of 3,450 students at participating institutions (2,309 service participants and 1,141 non-partici- pants) found "service effects strongest in the area of civic responsibility" (Sax and Astin, 1997: 28). Service participants were found to have stronger commitment to serving their community, more plans to volunteer in the future, and stronger commitments to promoting racial understanding, par- ticipating in community action, and influencing social values. A more recent Corporation for National Service program evaluation (Gray, Ondaatje, and Zakaras, 1999) found service-learning pos- itively associated with willingness to continue volunteer work and expectations to take an active role to address societal problems (8). Importantly, this study finds that the impact of service-learning increases significantly when service is closely integrated into overall course content (9). A more recent study of service-learning impacts based on a large sample of 22,236 undergraduates found positive impact on commitment to social activism and racial understanding (Astin et. al., 2000). This study also found evidence of the importance of active classroom reflection on service in the form of both class discussion and the professor making connections. Eyler and Giles, in a study based on a national survey and two rounds of in-depth interviews with a smaller group of students, found service-learn- ing associated with a greater sense of social responsibility, commitment to social justice, decreased stereotyping and increased tolerance, belief in the importance of volunteering, and connectedness to community (1999: 29–34; 156–163).

The problem with the evidence showing a correlation between service-learning and civic engagement lies in serious methodological weaknesses with almost all of the studies to date. The studies summarized thus far provide some tantalizing suggestions that community service and service-learning might make a difference for students' political and civic orientations. But their substantial weaknesses undermine any convincing claim that widespread service-learning will lead to a reversal of the civic disengagement among youth described earlier. Apart from the usual research problems of sample sizes, validity, and reliability of measures, nearly all share problems in the conceptualization of both "independent" and "dependent" variables. (See Cammarano, et al., 2000, for a more complete analysis.)

On the independent variable side, nearly all the studies cited suffer from an inadequate conceptualization of what is meant by community service and service-learning. This is especially a problem in those studies with the large sample sizes that, by necessity, must group together students involved in a large number of different programs. Respondents who report or are otherwise identified as experiencing service-learning are likely to have highly differential experiences, ranging from no connection between the service experience and the learning outcomes of the course (what Tim Stanton has called "parallel play" [Stanton, 1992]), to occasional out-of-class reflections linking service and learning, to classes in which readings, discussions, and lectures are tightly integrated with the service experience, all aimed at achieving concrete civic or political engagement ends. We cannot know what the impact that either community service or service-learning has on civic engagement unless research subjects are grouped clearly and we understand clearly what these groupings mean for the different educational experiences of the students. This is important not only for distinguishing among non-service, community service, and service-learning participants, but also for learning more about the impact of variations in the service-learning experience. In a recent essay, Hepburn, Niemi, and Chapman (2000), based on their review of existing literature, suggest that connection to course content, duration of service and intensity of relationships, and the character of in-class reflection are likely factors affecting service-learning impact. If this is so, then researchers must clarify carefully the nature of the service-learning experience being measured in each of these areas.

On the dependent variable side, many of the studies employ weak and indirect measures of civic or political impacts. Most civic impacts are described in terms of commitment to "community" or "social" responsibility, tolerance, or even the propensity to do further community service. Explicit political terminology seems eerily absent (see Walker, 2000a). One explanation may be that the researchers are not political scientists or that many of the studies look at civic engagement as a part of a larger study of service-learning impacts. Also, given that some of the most extensive research is funded by the Corporation for National Service or the U.S. Department of Education, researchers may hesitate to include explicit political language in questionnaires for fear of alienating congressional paymasters. Whatever the reason, researchers need to seek more direct and explicit measures of political involvement if we are to understand whether service-learning is an effective tool for civic education.

In the face of evidence pointing in different directions, what can be said beyond the fact that we need better and more extensive research? What the research suggests, and what my own experience confirms, is that civic learning does not *automatically* happen from a community service experience. In fact, without conscious attention to both the substantive issues addressed and the pedagogical strategies to be employed when engaging in service-learning, students merely engaging in service may come away as (or more) civically disengaged as the evidence suggests most are when they start participating in service-learning activities (for a qualified dissent, see Campbell, 2000). As John Dewey understood, the "discipline of experience" by itself may even be "miseducative," and therefore must always be subjected "to the tests of intelligent development and direction" (Dewey, 1938:89–90). The remainder of this book will make the case for service-learning as an effective vehicle in producing a more engaged and knowledgeable citizenry, but only when specific course characteristics are considered.

chapter two

Civic Engagement Across the Curriculum

At this point, those whose disciplines are chemistry or engineering, literature or theology, who teach in the business disciplines or in schools of education may be asking, Why Me? Service-learning tied to outcomes related to civic engagement may be appropriate for political or other social science disciplines, but what do I have to do with this concern over civic disengagement? It's hard enough for me to make connections between a community-based experience and the content of my courses. Now you want me to add a civic dimension? Why?

Well, another distinctive feature of the Campus Compact Presidents' Declaration, representative of the current emphasis in higher education, lies in the comprehensive scope of the effort to promote civic engagement. Higher education is currently talking about the "engaged campus," and is looking at all areas to accomplish the goal. The call to engage in service-learning for the purpose of creating a civically engaged student body and campus is one that increasingly touches all departments and disciplines at the institution. In this regard, a comparison can be made to previous efforts to do "writing across the curriculum." The movement for writing across the curriculum was based in an understanding that whatever a student's major or future aspiration, he or she needed to be proficient at written communication to be effective. This meant that every discipline or department at the university should concern itself with producing students who were "good writers." In a similar vein, the current movement toward "civic engagement" assumes that just as we want students to be good writers, we want them to be good citizens. Whatever the student's major, career, or life goals, she or he will be a member of some community, and for our democracy to be maintained and to flourish, we need people who will effectively exercise their civic rights and responsibilities. All faculty need to be enlisted in this effort to improve civic education.

This raises the question, what do we mean by "civic education?" What constitutes an effective education for citizenship? We must ask these questions if we are to be deliberate and intentional in seeking goals of civic learning for our students. However, while we might like to draw a parallel between civic engagement across the curriculum and writing across the curriculum, there is an immediate difference. Those in higher education who advocate "civic engagement across the curriculum" face an immediate disadvantage not faced by their counterparts who launched writing across the curriculum.

While there may be some disagreements, especially around the margins (no pun intended), about quality writing, there seems to be basic consensus around the question, "what is good writing?" The question of what constitutes "good citizenship," however, is highly controversial and contested. And the controversy surrounding definitions of good citizenship in part stems from the way citizenship is used in our schools. I can think of three contemporary areas where citizenship language actually serves as a barrier to positive conversations in the academy about education for civic engagement. First, citizenship is a legal status, a status not shared by all in our educational institutions. In fact, in states like California, where services like public education are tied to legal citizenship status, teachers are asked to serve as pseudo-agents of the Immigration and Naturalization Service. This exclusivity extends to the academic unit, where admonitions to faculty to be good "departmental citizens" over-look the differential status between "senior" and "junior," full- and part-time faculty members.

A second barrier to using the language of citizenship is ideological. Faculty on the left complain that citizenship education tends to convey images of patriotic flag-waving. More conservative faculty see civic engagement masking a leftist, activist agenda. Either way, the goal of civic engagement seems to lack academic and/or critical thinking substance, a charge to which service-learning is already subjected, without civic engagement as the ultimate goal!

Finally, the language of citizenship and civic engagement conjures up a childhood past that many faculty would just as soon forget, or at least would not endorse as characteristic of democratic life in a diverse society. Some of us remember our grade school "civics" courses as pedestrian and/or boring exercises. And for me, growing up in California, public schools gave "citizenship" grades on report cards based on a student's silence in the classroom, neatness, politeness, and passive obedience to school rules (I am told this still occurs in some school districts). When citizenship is tied to exclusive legal identities, ideologically charged language and symbols, or conformity to institutional norms, it is bound to raise suspicions, especially in the minds of academics.

Having said this, the language of citizenship also packs a kind of power not found in other language. We can find the image of democratic citizenship in the writings of Jefferson and Payne at the beginning of the Republic, and in the abolitionist and women's rights movements in the nineteenth century. Even those who have challenged our country's theories and institutions as too narrow or exclusive have found power in the language of democratic citizenship. For example, during the civil rights movement, the Southern Christian Leadership Council's first program was called "the crusade for Citizenship," focused on establishing "Citizenship Schools" in communities across the South. The primary purpose of the Citizenship Schools was to teach African-Americans to read and write, in order to pass literacy tests that had been devised to disenfranchise low-income people, particularly black citizens. But these schools went beyond instruction in literacy and voting rights to "talk about the meaning of American citizenship in ways that would inspire ordinary citizens" (Boyte, 1989: 67). The Student Nonviolent Coordinating Committee's "Freedom Schools" had similar aims, both in terms of black voter registration and in recasting understandings of democratic citizenship. Drawing on these historical traditions, democratic theorists like Barber (1984), Boyte (1989), and Rimmerman (1997) have all found meaning in this explicitly civic terminology. So with all of its negative baggage, the language of citizenship still offers great hope in our efforts to overcome youth disengagement.

While continuing to use the language of citizenship and civic education, we should feel free to challenge our conventional definitions of civic engagement. After all, citizenship is not a monolithic idea, to be defined narrowly or exclusively, forcing all in an institution to conform to a single standard. (Actually, I have used an exercise titled "How do you define citizenship?" that effectively makes this very point about contested definitions of citizenship—see Appendix A on page 71). There are multiple pathways to civic engagement, and if we want to encourage citizenship throughout the university and across the curriculum we need to leave room for multiple perspectives, even as we attempt to be deliberate in our efforts. In answering the question, "What is good citizenship?" we should begin with substantive, conceptual frameworks for civic education, then move on to the complement of skills and knowledge that a person should possess to be an effective citizen, particularly ones that might connect to disciplinary objectives or general education requirements.

The conceptual question is critical, yet sticky, wrapped up in issues surrounding fundamental values, definitions of citizenship, and tensions between personal/local/departmental and national identities. As exhibited in national studies, recent calls for educators to re-engage students as citizens generally assume a unified language of common-wealth, obscuring the realities and challenges of pluralism, both of values and identity. Students today are often suspicious of this language, and do not see any inherent connection between their service (producing a local identity) and their role as citizens (defined as a national identity). Faculty, too, become suspicious, because it denies them the opportunity to bring their perspectives—often disciplinary in nature—to bear on the question. Moreover, thoughtful attempts to incorporate broad-based definitions of citizenship—good for university-wide conversations—do not get specific enough for discipline-based academic units, where definitions need to be tied to concrete goals of each particular academic unit and faculty member in question. In examining the conceptual framework, then, it helps to look at different models of the democratic citizen, and what connections exist between a particular conceptual model, different academic disciplines, and the practice of service-learning.

chapter three

What Is Good Citizenship?
CONCEPTUAL FRAMEWORKS IN THE SOCIAL SCIENCES

There are a number of different conceptual frameworks of civic engagement/citizenship developed by political and social theorists, all of which lend themselves—albeit in different ways—to corresponding outcomes for service-learning and civic education. I will be taking up five of these frameworks here, as an illustration of the variety of ways social theorists conceive of citizenship. These frameworks may share some common themes, but they are distinct enough to offer separate conceptions of the democratic citizen, with corresponding skills that the citizen under each model would need to develop. A matrix comparing each framework's perspective on citizenship, civic education, and the associated civic skills needed for effective public life follows the narrative summary (see Figure 1 on page 17).

Constitutional Citizenship
What I call constitutional citizenship—others use the terms "liberal" or "civics" to define this approach—begins with the individual and focuses on the individual's rights and interests. The role of politics and government is to secure individuals' rights and interests, to provide the laws and services necessary for a functioning, orderly society. But under this conception, there are limits to what the public realm can provide, and dangers lurking in allowing the government too much authority. The "good citizen" is one who knows and upholds the laws and the basic political institutions of the society, understanding that internalizing certain rules and standards of public behavior is useful in providing for the orderly accommodation of private wishes in the public realm. Beyond knowing and obeying the Constitution and the laws, good citizenship involves political participation to the extent necessary to provide for the individuals' particular interests: voting for public officials who will represent them in public affairs and joining interest groups or lobbying for legislation that accords with their interests and values. But participation in the public realm does not define the role of the citizen under this conceptual model. Political participation is not a self-fulfilling or even a necessary activity; as long as one's private interests are represented one need not act any further in the public realm—in fact, such additional activity is foolish (see Madison, 1961: 315; Rawls, 1971: 227–28; Lippmann, 1922: 195–97).

The Harwood Group report *College Students Talk Politics* complained that the students they interviewed largely held this "narrow" view of politics and citizenship (Harwood Group, 1993: 42). Nevertheless, service-learning is certainly consistent with this approach to citizenship. Community service becomes the actions of individuals building a strong civil society that takes care of the rights and interests of all, volunteer activity that provides what government cannot. For faculty, reflection on service can bring out conversations about public and private, voluntary action versus public policy making.

Communitarianism

Where the focus of constitutional citizenship is on individual rights and interests, the focus of communitarian citizenship is the "social dimension of human existence" (Etzioni, 1994: 253). In fact, communitarians believe that we suffer from an overemphasis on individual rights to the detriment of collective responsibilities, and seek to rectify what they see as an improper balance between rights and responsibilities. Concerned about the moral fabric underlying the political order, the communitarian wants to build a consensus about the values that should undergird law and other rules of the social order. Given this perspective, the role of citizen is not only to exercise rights, but to learn about the community's values, commit to their articulation, and to discharge the responsibilities that come from adherence to these values and the laws or needs that follow from them. Citizenship involves sharing (community values), commitment (to others in the community and to the values shared) and caring (for others in the community).

Communitarians have consistently supported community service and service-learning as an embodiment of their conception of citizenship. For communitarians, service deemed useful to communities not only represents the orientation they have toward community good over private interests and rights, but also reflects the responsibilities that individuals owe to the larger community that accompany the rights they enjoy. Moreover, to the extent that service-learning is connected to moral and character education, it allows students to learn the set of shared values held by the larger community (see Etzioni, 1994: 113–114).

Participatory Democracy

Its current embodiment in theorists such as Benjamin Barber (1984; 1992) and Meta Mendel-Reyes (1995) draws historical inspiration from a theory and practice going all the way back to ancient Athens. Like communitarians, participatory democrats stress the "crucial democratic relationship between rights and responsibilities" (Barber, 1992: 254). But from this perspective the most important of these citizen responsibilities (and rights) is that of actively participating in the decisions that affect our collective lives. Advocates of participatory democracy believe that democratic self-governance is not a spectator sport, and that the purpose of civic education is to prepare young people for a life of public participation.

From the participatory democratic perspective, community service has value, not as an end in itself, but as a tool of democratic civic education. Benjamin Barber puts it this way:

Idea of Social contract

Service is something we owe to ourselves or to that part of ourselves that is embedded in the civic community. It assumes that our rights and liberties are not acquired for free; that unless we assume the responsibilities of citizens, we will not be able to preserve the liberties they entail. …Where students use experience in the community as a basis for critical reflection in the classroom, and turn classroom reflection into a tool to examine the nature of democratic communities and the role of the citizen in them, there is an opportunity to teach liberty, to uncover the interdependence of self and other, to expose the intimate linkage between rights and responsibilities.

—Barber, 1992: 246, 252

From this perspective, service-learning courses offer an opportunity for students to connect their work in communities to ideas about more active participation as citizens in a democracy.

"Public Work"

The concept of "public work" is most associated with Harry Boyte and his colleagues at the University of Minnesota. Boyte has consciously tried to distinguish citizenship as public work from both the liberal and communitarian understandings of politics and civic engagement. Public work shares with participatory democracy a concern with involving all the people in the decisions that affect their public life, and the critique of constitutional citizenship as overly privatized, not capturing the things people share in common. But where Boyte and others distinguish their views of civic engagement from communitarians and participatory democrats lies in the words public and work. The word public is to be distinguished from community, as community often implies a spirit of moral agreement. ← Boyte argues that "the people" who make up the citizenry must be conceived as coming from different backgrounds, with different experiences, and "contending versions of morality" (Boyte & Kari, 1996: p.28). People come together to identify and solve important public problems (i.e., ones that cannot be solved privately), but with the understanding that there will be disagreement about the ends of politics. Moreover, "work" is stressed because it captures the creative and productive role for democratic citizenship (as opposed to the role of citizen as consumer, client, or volunteer). Democratic civic engagement is about more than process; it represents the "work of the people, creating public things" (Boyte, 2000: 70).

The concept of public work has been associated with a particular form of youth community service. Often critical of traditional community service, which they feel reinforces the notion of citizen as volunteer or client, public work theorists begin by conceiving young people as "creators and producers," *collaborators* as opposed to "community servants." This means that a program involving community-based activity must begin with the young people themselves defining the very problems that they will set about to solve in their communities. The signature service-learning program exemplifying a public work perspective has been Public Achievement, a program begun at the University of Minnesota in 1990. In Public Achievement, undergraduate students enrolled in service-learning courses serve as "coaches" to teams of elementary, middle, or high school students who themselves work to devise and implement projects addressing some public issue that the students have identified. Thus, in a twofold process of experiential activity, K-12 students work collectively to solve public problems that they have identified, and as a result, learn "how to co-create and function in democratic groups." In turn, the undergraduate students who "serve" as coaches to these younger students "learn about themselves as citizens as they undergo training, coach youth, participate in debriefing sessions with fellow coaches, keep journals, complete readings, and take part in class discussions" (see Hildreth, 2000: 627–32; Boyte, 2000).

Social Capital

In recent years, the concept of social capital has been most associated with the work of Robert Putnam (1993, 1995, 2000), but its contemporary origins reach to earlier work by sociologist James Coleman (Coleman, 1988; 1990; Coleman & Kilgore, 1987), and draws inspiration from the study by Alexis de Tocqueville of *Democracy in America* (Tocqueville, 1945). In his travels across the United States in the 1820s, Tocqueville observed that "Americans of all ages, all stations in life, and all types of disposition are forever forming associations" outside of politics in the voluntary sector of civil society. He argued that this propensity to form and build networks of voluntary association helped counteract the isolating effects of American individualism, and was one of the reasons for the strength of American democracy. Following in Tocqueville's footsteps, Robert Putnam has recently published a study—titled *Bowling Alone*—which reveals a steady and precipitous decline over the past forty years in our propensity to join associations, and along with it a corresponding decline in political activity, knowledge, and attitudes of public trust and efficacy (Putnam, 2000). While social capitalists like Putnam might agree with advocates of participatory democracy or public work on the importance of involvement in public life, from their perspective, civic engagement involves more than participation in the political arena. It requires that citizens rebuild the social institutions of civil society that can create the networks of social connectedness between people that bolster all aspects of community life.

Those who argue that civic engagement involves building social capital see education-based community service as a particularly appropriate strategy for social change, "especially if the service is meaningful, regular, and woven into the fabric of the school curriculum" (Putnam, 2000: 405). Social capitalists believe that community service increases the kind of voluntary participation in the institutions/associations of civil society that Tocqueville deemed so important to the development of American democracy. It has the effect, according to David Campbell, of "thickening [the] bonds of social connectedness among students and between students and adults within their community" (Campbell, 2000: 644). Moreover, as a pedagogy, service-learning is seen as one vehicle that can be used to enhance the civic education and attitudes of young people—whose political participation has been in decline for over two decades—thus paving the way for increased political participation.

Conceptual Frameworks from the Social Sciences

Conceptual Framework	View of Citizenship	Understanding of Civic Education	Associated Civic Skills (see Ch. 5)	Disciplinary Affinities
Constitutional Citizenship	Rights-bearing individual; voter	Learning about governmental institutions, laws, elections	Political Knowledge Critical Thinking	Political Science Law Policy Studies (e.g., health, education)
Communitar-ianism	"Good neighbor" duty to fulfill common good	Learning about community values and civic responsibilities	Civic Judgment Community Building	Philosophy Religious Studies Social Work
Participatory Democracy	Active participant in public life	Learning the processes of democratic participation	Communication Skills Collective Action Civic Imagination	Political Science Education
Public Work	Co-creator of things of public value	Learning through projects about the skills, practices, habits, and values of working with others on public tasks	Public Problem Solving Coalition Building	Political Science Public Administration Prof. Disciplines
Social Capital	Membership in associations of civil society	Learning about social connections and institutions	Communication Skills Organizational Analysis	Sociology Not-For-Profit Management

chapter four

What Is Good Citizenship?
CONCEPTUAL CONTRIBUTIONS FROM OTHER DISCIPLINES

The five conceptual frameworks I have just outlined give an example of how social scientists have answered the question of citizenship and how faculty might tie conceptions of citizenship to service-learning. If we want to engage all across campus in education for civic engagement, however, we need to go beyond the social sciences for conceptual frameworks that will inform the theory and practice of service-learning. While political and other social scientists have a rich tradition and language around concepts like democracy, citizenship, community, political participation, civil society, and public work, they obviously do not own these concepts, and given the evidence of declining political participation (especially among young people), they may not be communicating it very effectively or in a way that resonates with students. In fact, the more we engage in narrow or rhetorical definitions of service and citizenship, the more we may turn away both students and faculty—especially those outside the social science disciplines. This calls at once for all disciplines, which may have equally effective conceptual frameworks, to join into the discourse around a multidisciplinary civic education. To paraphrase a statement made by Vaclav Havel in one of his first New Year's Addresses as president of the Czech Republic, the public problems we face as a people are such that require the collaboration of "well-rounded people," those informed by a variety of perspectives and conceptual frameworks (Havel, 1997: 9).

In this spirit, more than a year ago I began a conversation with representatives from a number of different disciplinary associations about the language and conceptual frameworks that resonated with their own disciplines. Out of this initial conversation, I generated the following list of terms:

- social capital
  (or social trust)

- civic engagement

- civic responsibility

- citizenship

- democracy/democratic citizenship/
  democratic participation

- democratic practice

- public or community problem solving

- the creation of a public

- "public intellectual"
- civic professionalism
- corporate/institutional citizenship
- social responsibility, social accountability (or public accountability)
- social issues
- social justice
- public agency, public capacity
- social ethics, civic ethics, public ethics
- public scholarship
- community identity
- community responsibility
- community building
- common ground

- altruism
- prosocial behavior
- reciprocity
- civic or public leadership
- the creation of "public intellectuals"
- civic obligation
- public life
- other-regardingness
- creation of a more democratic society
- civil society
- the not-for-profit sector
- preparation for multicultural/intercultural citizenship
- community partnerships

The list was whittled down, based on positive faculty responses, to the following seven conceptual frameworks for civic engagement that come from theory and practice found in disciplines outside the social sciences. While certainly not exhaustive of the possibilities, these frameworks may better lend themselves to integrating service-learning into the civic engagement curriculum for many faculty than those found in the social sciences. As with the preceding chapter, a matrix comparing the answers each framework brings to the question of citizenship, civic education, the associated civic skills needed for effective public life, along with each framework's disciplinary affinities, follows the narrative summary (see Figure 2 on page 29).

Civic Professionalism

In discussing the concept of civic professionalism I draw primarily from the argument made by William Sullivan in his book *Work and Integrity* (Sullivan, 1995). Sullivan, a philosopher by discipline and one of the co-authors of *Habits of the Heart* and *The Good Society,* traces the ideal of professionalism and professional work to the social reformers writing at the turn of the twentieth century. Sullivan contends that under this ideal, professional work was characterized by three central features:

- specialized training in a field of codified knowledge usually acquired by formal education and apprenticeship,

- public recognition of a certain autonomy on the part of the community of practitioners to regulate their own standards of practice,

- and a commitment to provide service to the public which goes beyond the economic welfare of the practitioners.

—Sullivan, 2

In fact, the three features were originally thought to be intimately related to each other. The professional drew her social status, and the concomitant financial rewards, from her technical knowledge and expertise. This expertise also bought the professional autonomy in the workplace, something deemed critical to job satisfaction. In exchange, the professional was conceived as owing something back to the society from whom she drew this status and autonomy. So as a kind of *quid pro quo,* professionals were expected to contribute their knowledge to the public: indirectly, through their deliberations over matters of civic concern; and directly, through *pro bono* work with disadvantaged citizens. Originally referring to those working in the "classic honorific occupations of medicine, the bar, and the clergy," the status of professional was extended broadly to include fields such as business, education, engineering, governmental bureaucracy, health care (beyond physicians), architecture, and planning. But Sullivan asserts that while professionalization has grown tremendously over the past century, its connection to the "culture of civic democracy" emblematic of the third feature of professional work has weakened severely. While professional work has risen in social status and desirability, the civic responsibility that was originally understood as the price a professional paid for social and economic recognition and personal autonomy has declined. What we are witnessing today, according to Sullivan, is a professional ethic where technical expertise has become decoupled from civic purpose.

Sullivan argues that we must revitalize the civic orientation that originally stood at the foundation of the professions. In the United States, where the professions "pioneered and continue to model a socially attuned way to organize work," (Sullivan, 222), we need civically minded professionals more than ever. Clearly, the challenges that face our society today require even more professional expertise than those confronted by citizens during the Progressive era. "Few kinds of work would seem better fitted to these needs of the new era than professions with a civic orientation" (Sullivan, 237). In particular, Sullivan calls upon professional education to re-instill the civic dimension that seems lacking in contemporary discussions of professional ethics and integrity.

This concept of civic professionalism should have great resonance in a number of fields where service-learning has been used as a pedagogy. Professional school educators who already deploy community service as a method of teaching concepts and practices in disciplinary courses could expand service-learning to explore related civic themes. With this concept in mind, students engaged in curriculum-based community service in schools of business, education, engineering, the health professions, law, and planning could be encouraged to reflect on the civic dimensions of their anticipated work. (For some examples of reflection questions that tap civic dimensions see Appendix B on page 72.)

Social Responsibility

Where civic responsibility may be a concept that needs reviving, social responsibility is a well-established idea in a number of professions. We now see organizations devoted to connecting professional work with social responsibility in such fields as medicine, business, computer technology, architecture, and planning.

One of the first and most well-known organizations pushing this approach is Physicians for Social Responsibility (PSR). Begun during the Cold War in 1961, PSR originated with an understanding that all doctors have an ethical as well as a professional responsibility to work toward the elimination of violence—with an original emphasis on curbing nuclear weapons—global environmental degradation, and social and economic inequities. Part of this ethic of the physicians' social responsibility involves civic engagement: one of the central values of PSR is that "citizens have a right to informed participation in such decision-making processes made by both government and industry which affect their health, welfare, and environment" (www.psr.org/aboutpsr.htm).

Other organizations have followed the lead of PSR. Business for Social Responsibility has the mission of "providing members with innovative products and services that help companies be commercially successful in ways that demonstrate respect for ethical values, people, communities, and the environment" (www.bsr.org). Computer Professionals for Social Responsibility declares itself to be "a public interest alliance of computer scientists and others concerned about the impact of computer technology on society" (www.cpsr.org).

Faculty members—particularly those in disciplines which prepare students for professions with corresponding "social responsibility" arms—might see this idea of social responsibility as a natural pathway to a form of civic engagement. For example, as part of a service-learning course that's a required component of premedical education, students could be directed to the PSR literature and website as one of the tools for reflection on their service. A local representative from PSR could be invited in to discuss with students the social responsibilities of people entering the medical profession. And these connections would be enhanced even further if the community service connected to the course were in the specific areas addressed by PSR, such as peace and nonviolence, the environment, or public health. (See Placement Quality section that follows.)

Social Justice

Notions of social justice may also provide powerful connections to civic engagement for faculty, particularly those teaching in faith-based institutions of higher education. While numerous definitions of social justice exist, David Hollenbach offers one of the better ones, connecting social justice—as developed in the context of the social teachings of the Catholic Church—and civic engagement:

> It refers to the obligations of all citizens to aid in the creation of patterns of social organization and activity that are essential both for the protection of minimal human rights and for the creation of mutuality and participation by all in social life.
>
> —Hollenbach, 1988: 27

A similar understanding can be found in the American Catholic bishops' pastoral letter on the economy:

> Social justice implies that persons have an obligation to be active and productive participants in the life of society and that society has a duty to enable them to participate in this way.

—National Conference of Catholic Bishops, 1986: 36

The logic of this framework is that social justice moves individuals to work in active solidarity with fellow human beings to seek the common good of all who live in their community. Under this conception, then, a just individual is necessarily a good citizen.

A social justice framework has much to recommend itself. Not only does it offer a powerful nonpolitical path to civic engagement (important given the current student turnoff from traditional politics as documented at the outset of this book). Additionally, for faculty teaching service-learning courses at faith-based colleges and universities, this perspective can provide a seamless link between student service, the specific subject matter of their courses, the institution's mission, and civic engagement.

There exists a growing body of literature connecting faith, justice, and citizenship, usually tied to specific faith traditions and texts. To give just one example, the Catholic social justice tradition contains within it a principle known as "subsidiarity." Subsidiarity requires, on the one hand, that problems be solved and decisions be made at the smallest level of association. The assumption is that smaller communities—local not-for-profit organizations, churches, civic groups—can more effectively and compassionately address the needs of their people, and that a distant, often unresponsive federal government or multinational business enterprise should therefore not usurp or replace the authority of the smaller body to act on behalf of its members. But the principle of subsidiarity also holds that when "the demands of justice exceed the capacities" of the smaller/local units, then government has an affirmative duty to act in solving social problems (National Conference of Catholic Bishops, 1986: 62). Teaching at Providence College, I have successfully introduced subsidiarity as a way of engaging my students who do community service from their faith backgrounds in conversations about politics and public problem solving. The principle of subsidiarity also fits nicely with discussions of mediating institutions and social capital formation (see discussion, page 16), and with basic principles of grass roots community organizing, especially the efforts sponsored by the Industrial Areas Foundation, a network of community-based organizations that teach citizens in local neighborhoods how to work together effectively to achieve public ends (see Rogers, 1990; Fischer, 1997).

More generally, social justice is a conceptual framework that can help faculty in terms of guiding students' reflection on their service. A social justice perspective can help move service-learners from the "personal" that often characterizes service to the "political," because a "foundation in social justice requires that community service from a faith perspective move beyond charity and address the root causes that create the need for service within our society and world" (Swezey, 1990: 78). It also allows faculty to ask the question, "How do/will you incorporate social justice and service into your daily lives?"—an opening to increased civic engagement. Social justice frameworks can provide ties between course-based service-learning and co-curricular efforts of campus ministry offices. And finally, a social justice perspective complements reciprocal approaches to community partnerships:

> Paramount to the quest for justice is the building of authentic relationships between students and the individuals and communities with whom they serve. These relationships affirm the reciprocal learning inherent in service. Service in this context is not a doing to or for but a service with a person or group; enabling and empowering disenfranchised individuals and communities to be "agents of their own development and not just the beneficiaries of someone else's efforts." Together, the student and the individuals or communities being served plan and carry out the community service experience. The task of the service becomes secondary to the relationships that develop within the service experience.
>
> —Swezey, 1990: 87

(For more on community partnerships consistent with democratic civic engagement, see the section on Community Voice in chapter seven).

Connected Knowing; "Ethic of Care"

Faculty coming into service-learning from a feminist perspective may find pathways to civic engagement through the literature on "connected knowing" or "caring" as a social ethic. Building on the work of Carol Gilligan (1982), Belenky, Clinchy, Goldberger, & Tarule (1986) developed the concept of "connected knowing" as a way of describing a "proclivity toward thinking" they found in undergraduate women, to be contrasted from the dominant understanding of how we ought to think, what they call "separate knowing." The critical distinction between the two kinds of thinking, they argue, lies in whether we see ourselves as dispassionately detached or empathetically connected to the object known (and by extension to other "knowing beings"):

> The separate knower holds herself aloof from the object she is trying to analyze. She takes an impersonal stance. She follows certain rules or procedures to ensure that her judgments are unbiased.... Separate knowing often takes the form of an adversarial proceeding. The separate knower's primary mode of discourse is the argument.
>
> Connected knowers are not dispassionate, unbiased observers. They deliberately bias themselves in favor of what they are examining. They try to get inside it and form an intimate attachment to it. The heart of connected knowing is imaginative attachment: trying to get behind the other person's eyes and "look at it from that person's point of view."
>
> —Clinchy, 1989

Based upon the research into women's ways of knowing, feminist thinkers have called upon institutions of higher education to value connected knowing, to be places where "people are encouraged to think about the things that they care about and to care about the things they think about" (Clinchy, 1989).

Speaking of "care," there also abounds in the feminist literature discussions of an "ethic of care," not only to describe the way women's engagement with others has been characterized, but also as a political ethic to be embraced (Noddings, 1984). Joan Tronto (1993:103) defines "care" as human activity "that includes everything that we do to maintain, continue, and repair our 'world' so that we can live in it as well as possible. That world includes our bodies, our selves, and our environment, all of which we seek to interweave in a complex, life-sustaining web."

While the gendered origins or associations of connected knowing and/or caring can be contested, there should be no doubt that the feminist orientation toward knowledge and caring can be a powerful way of moving from personal to civic engagement. And this conceptual framework lends itself to the pedagogy of service-learning. Not only does much of community service work come out of the "caring professions," but a student's course-related service can be reflected through the conceptual lens of "caring." This even allows the community service connected to a course to be subjected to various critiques of "care" as a concept that may be oppressive to women particularly when service-learning programs or courses are disproportionately populated by women, as is the case on many campuses. (For an example of a service-learning course reflecting this conceptual framework, taught by a faculty member in philosophy, see Foos, 2000.)

Public Leadership

At first blush, concepts associated with "leadership" would not seem to be compatible with notions of democratic citizenship. After all, "leaders" usually produce "followers," and the characteristics of followers appear on the surface to be inconsistent with those of the engaged citizen. In the U.S. context, Benjamin Barber has gone so far as to argue that "strong leaders have on the whole made Americans weak citizens…the conditions and consequences of leadership often seem to undermine civic vigor" (Barber, 1999: 164–5).

There are, however, rich conceptions of public leadership that compliment understandings of engaged democratic citizenship. In fact, we can trace ideas about this kind of "transformational" democratic leadership at least as far back as Rousseau's *Social Contract,* with more contemporary versions found in the writings of John Dewey, James MacGregor Burns, and Saul Alinsky (see Dewey, 1916; Burns, 1979; Alinsky, 1969). Burns puts the reciprocal relationship between leaders and citizens in a democracy this way:

> Leadership is not a surrogate for participation in a democracy, it is its necessary condition. Without leaders, a citizenry is unlikely to remain active; without active citizens, responsive leaders are unlikely to emerge, and leaders who do emerge are unlikely to remain responsive.

> —Burns, 1979: 439

Viewed this way, then, a leadership framework can be yet another pathway to engaged citizenship. And given the emergence of "leadership studies" as a growing area on college campuses—not only in business disciplines but as an interdisciplinary field on its own—connecting the study of public leadership to civic engagement may make sense. Moreover, recent philosophies of "steward" or "servant" leadership have strong connections with service-learning, and can serve as bridges between leadership studies, community-based learning, and civic education (see Greenleaf, 1996; see also the Greenleaf Center for Servant-Leadership, at http://www.greenleaf.org. A good example of a university-based leadership program, one with strong service-learning connections, is the Jepson School of Leadership Studies at the University of Richmond; see: http://www.richmond.edu/academics/leadership).

The Public Intellectual

So far, the different conceptual models of citizenship offered tend heavily toward the social sciences and pre-professional disciplines. To the extent that we might find connections to the humanities, it would be primarily philosophers or theologians who see concepts that resonate with their disciplines. There may be little conceptually for those in literature of the arts to latch on to, leading to the question, "What does citizenship have to do with us?" My conversations with faculty in the literary, visual, and performing arts suggest that the tradition of the "public intellectual" or the artist inspired to contribute to a political vision may be a powerful pathway to civic engagement in these fields.

What is meant by the term "public intellectual?" Simply put, public intellectuals are writers, artists, and thinkers "who address a general and educated audience…who contribute to open discussions" (Jacoby, 1987: 5, 221). They are women and men of intellect or vision who are not content to share their work with a specialized, esoteric audience, but bring the power of their ideas to bear on the public problems or questions of the day. In a democracy particularly, where majorities and public opinion rule, it has been thought critical to society's growth and progress to have a class of people who can contribute their ideas and vision to general public discourse. Writing in the nineteenth century, Walt Whitman makes this case for such a contribution to democracy in the United States:

> Our fundamental want today in the United States, with closest, amplest reference to present conditions, and to the future, is of a class, and the clear idea of a class, of native authors, literatuses, far different, far higher in grade than any yet known, sacerdotal, modern, fit to cope with our occasions, lands, permeating the whole mass of American mentality, taste, belief, breathing into it a new breath of life, giving it decision, affecting politics far more than the popular superficial suffrage, with results inside and underneath the elections of Presidents or Congresses—radiating, begetting appropriate teachers, schools, manners, and, as its grandest result, accomplishing (what neither the schools nor the churches and their clergy have hitherto accomplish'd, and without which this nation will no more stand, permanently, soundly, than a house will stand without a substratum,) a religious and moral character beneath the political and productive and intellectual bases of the States.
>
> —Walt Whitman

Following Shelley, who called poets "the unacknowledged legislators of the world," Whitman believed that American poets, writers, artists, and thinkers had a duty to contribute to the public discourse, to "become the justification and reliance of American democracy" (Whitman, 1999: 49). This tradition of public intellectuals in the United States would carry from Whitman, Ralph Waldo Emerson, Herbert Melville, Margaret Fuller, and Mark Twain in the nineteenth century to such individuals as Herbert Croly, John Dewey, Langston Hughes, Walter Lippmann, and Frank Capra in the early decades of the twentieth century (for examples of modern artists who have served the function of public intellectual, see Barber & McGrath, 1982).

The concept of a public intellectual may seem antiquated to many today. Indeed, a number of scholars would argue that the public intellectual is a dying breed, owing to changes in the media and popular culture, university life and work, and the demands of modern science and technology (see Bender, 1993; Jacoby, 1987; Hollander, et al., 2001). Still, this is a conceptual framework that may resonate with faculty in the humanities (for an extension to economists, see Levine, 2001), offering a number of natural links to service-learning. Students engaged in literary or artistic service projects can be introduced to this tradition of civic engagement through written texts and other works of public or political art. This conceptual tradition can be tied to the skills of civic imagination and creativity, with course assignments designed to make explicit linkage between literature or art and public value (see section, pages 36–37).

The Scholarship of Engagement, Public Scholarship

As noted in the last section, the notion of the "public intellectual" may seem antiquated to many faculty, the product of a bygone era. In the past decade, many faculty, especially those involved in experiential or service-learning, resonate more deeply to notions of engaged or public scholarship. The idea of connecting academic scholarship to engagement owes much to Ernest Boyer. In a 1996 essay, Boyer claimed that higher education needed to "become a more vigorous partner in the search for answers to our most pressing social, civic, economic, and moral problems, and must reaffirm its historic commitment to what I call the scholarship of engagement." Building on his report for the Carnegie Foundation for the Advancement of Teaching, entitled *Scholarship Reconsidered,* Boyer argued that "the scholarship of engagement means connecting the rich resources of the university to our most pressing social, civic, and ethical problems" (Boyer, 1996: 11–20). A number of scholars have built upon Boyer's foundations, making the case for the civic purposes of academic research and scholarship (see Benson and Harkavy, 1997; Checkoway, 2001). The American Association for Higher Education's Forum on Faculty Roles and Rewards has advanced these notions of "engaged scholarship," and AAHE has published a number of resources for faculty interested in connecting advanced scholarship with public purposes (see their website, at: http://www.aahe.org/FFRR/).

As a variation on the theme of engaged scholarship, Jeremy Cohen has recently offered what he thinks is a more civically minded conceptual framework for the research work done by faculty and students: public scholarship. According to Cohen, public scholarship gives both faculty and students the opportunity to "imagine their academic capacity as a way to contribute as citizen participants, in a community structure where their intellectual decisions do make a difference." As Cohen defines it,

> public scholarship as an approach assumes a duty to make university scholarship public and to use our discoveries in the interest of the community....The social act of public scholarship itself provides a laboratory in which students can view their work not as the isolated, self-indulged actions of a campus segregated from society, but as the contributions of citizens with membership in a larger community.
>
> —Cohen, 2001: 15–16

This conceptual approach lends itself to a different kind of community service: "participatory action research" conducted by students and their faculty in collaboration with their community partners. Under this model, community-based organizations identify research projects that would contribute to their work, and universities—through service-learning curricula—provide their research resources as a form of service. Seen this way, service-learning as engaged or public scholarship can be a vehicle for faculty and students to reflect upon the public purposes of academic research, and the civic responsibilities of academic institutions. At Stanford, for example, the Haas Center for Public Service offers a "Senior Honors Research in Public Service Seminar," a full-year course that "provides an organizational structure to encourage and support participants committed to developing a thesis that meets criteria for academic excellence and also realizes the program's theme and goal, 'research as a form of public service'" (Cruz, 1998). Academic programs at the institutions such as the University of Pennsylvania and the University of Illinois are grounded in this approach (see Harkavy, 2000; Reardon, 1997).

Conceptual Frameworks in Other Disciplines

Conceptual Framework	View of Citizenship	Understanding of Civic Education	Associated Civic Skills (see Ch. 5)	Disciplinary Affinities
Civic Professionalism	Professional work with a civic purpose	Learning about the civic traditions and values of the professions	Public Problem Solving Civic Judgment	Professional Disciplines
Social Responsibility	Responsibility to larger society	Learning about the public problems most closely associated with chosen field of work	Political Knowledge (Issues) Organizational Analysis	Health Professions Business Disciplines Computer Science
Social Justice	Bringing one's spiritual values to bear on social problems	Learning the principles of social justice and their application to public life	Civic Judgment Collective Action	Religious Studies Philosophy Faith-Based Institutions
Connected Knowing; Ethic of Care	Caring for the future of our public world	Learning about others and their perspectives on the world	Critical Thinking Coalition Building	Women's Studies Psychology Nursing
Public Leadership	Citizen as "servant-leader"	Learning the arts of collaborative leadership	Community Building Communication	Management Leadership Studies
Public Intellectual	Thinkers who contribute to the public discourse	Learning about the traditions of writers and artists who have served as public intellectuals	Civic Imagination & Creativity	Literature Visual & Performing Arts
Engaged/Public Scholarship	Participatory action researcher	Learning about how scholarly research might contribute to the needs and values of the community	Organizational Analysis Public Problem Solving	Journalism Communications Professional Disciplines Land Grant Instit.

chapter five

Beyond Conceptual Frameworks:
THE PRACTICAL SKILLS OF ENGAGED CITIZENSHIP

We now have a sampling of conceptual models that can inform a faculty member's integration of civic education into their work in service-learning. But we must move beyond abstract notions of citizenship if we are to make a strong case about the connections between service-learning and an empowered citizenry. We must also discuss the concrete skills that people need to be effective citizens. Here I will focus on several sets of civic skills that can be incorporated into service-learning courses regardless of the disciplinary focus. As you will see, in most cases the skills addressed are those that traditionally have been defined as part of a "liberal education" (see Cronon, 1999). They also represent skills that increasingly are being incorporated into disciplinary and professional standards for accreditation.

Political Knowledge and Critical Thinking Skills

As with other areas of the curriculum, intellectual understanding cannot be shortchanged. Since 1893, when a "Committee of Ten" leading American educators produced a report which said that the chief purpose of education was "to train the mind," the main thrust of American education at all levels has been cognitive development. In civic education, this begins with the transmission of political knowledge, the basic facts and structures of government. The possession of political knowledge is obviously a central civic skill. It has long been understood that citizens armed with factual information about politics are more effective, more capable of connecting policy positions to core values, and generally more supportive of critical democratic values such as tolerance (Delli Carpini and Keeter, 1996).

But cognitive civic skills go well beyond the learning of political facts and figures; they must include the ability to think critically about substantive political issues. We want to develop citizens who can use a variety of methods, theories, and models to examine the world and evaluate facts, in order to reach conclusions.

How does service-learning relate to these two cognitive civic skills? In the case of political knowledge, some might question the connection. Many political scientists, for example, have dismissed service-learning, believing that there is a tradeoff between time spent learning essential political facts and time doing community service and/or reflecting on its relevance to civic participation. Recently, however, Michael Delli Carpini and Scott Keeter have urged educators to rethink this equation, understanding that

> political learning is more likely to occur when the information is directly relevant to one's immediate circumstances and behaviors. It is likely that a service learning experience, properly constituted, could activate interest and demonstrate relevance in ways that would increase a student's receptivity to and retention of factual knowledge....Well-designed service learning projects would expose students to a great deal of essential contextual information about substantive issues, key political actors, the law, policy making, political participation (and the barriers thereto), and other fundamentals of the operation of the political system, all of which would increase the likelihood of political learning.
>
> —Delli Carpini and Keeter, 2000

Note, however, their constant reference to "properly constituted" and "well-designed" service-learning activities. Implicit in their advocacy of service-learning as a route to the acquisition of political knowledge is the warning that the connection between the two is wholly related to both the nature of the community service experience and its integration into the classroom.

As an example, in the fall of 2000 my colleague Joe Cammarano and I revamped our introductory American Government course to include a service-learning component. In this course, students chose from several service options designed to give them a deeper experience of elections in the United States. Most students enrolled in the three sections of the course we taught worked as "Democracy Captains" for an organization called the Democracy Compact, a statewide, grassroots effort to increase citizen participation in the 2000 election. Student captains were leaders responsible for recruiting other students to register and vote, either in Rhode Island or by absentee ballot in their home states. (The Democracy Compact effort at Providence College was wildly successful, with a 300 percent increase in voter turnout over 1996 at the primary Providence College polling place on campus!) But we didn't merely incorporate community service options like this one into the design of an already existing course. Student participation in this and other election-oriented service was tightly integrated into a revised curriculum, through class discussions, readings, and written reflection assignments, enhancing students' understanding of government, elections, and arguments about the civic disengagement of youth in the political process. In particular, students working on the Democracy Compact effort had to learn about laws and policies regarding voter registration, including residency requirements, absentee voting procedures, and restrictions on voter eligibility. Our efforts that semester further convinced us of the need to be intentional in the design of any service-learning experience (see Placement Quality and Application/Reflection issues on pages 53–54).

Similarly, service-learning can enhance the development of students' critical thinking skills, and experiences in the community can reveal challenges to their working cognitive assumptions regarding human nature, society, and justice. Students' ability to analyze critically is enhanced by confronting ideas and theories with the actual realities in the world surrounding them. For example, I have placed students in service experiences working with guests in homeless shelters, and they have reported that they were both able to put a face on "the poor" and to test their own and others' theories about poverty, public policy, and democracy against their actual observations and the real life stories of those with whom they interacted in the shelters.

Communication Skills

Intellectual understanding, while essential to democratic citizenship, must be accompanied by what I would call "participation skills," and one of the most important of these is communication. Communication skills are essential to effective civic participation, and to the values of civility and public deliberation. In addition to clear thinking about public matters, democratic citizenship involves the communication of our thoughts and actions, both vertically, to our leaders and representatives, and horizontally, with our fellow citizens. Speech, argument, and persuasive communication all are important elements of democratic literacy. Perhaps even more important is the lost art of listening. In a democracy, citizens need to be able to listen to each other, to understand the places and interests of others in the community, and to achieve compromises and solve problems when conflict occurs. The overriding images of our democratic culture tend to involve talkers: great communicators like Thomas Jefferson, Daniel Webster, Martin Luther King, and Ronald Reagan; representatives giving speeches or talking on C-SPAN; or lawyers persuasively arguing in the courtroom. Perhaps the truer image of democracy exists on the other side of the courtroom, among the members of the jury, both listening to the arguments and testimony and to each other in deliberation. An effective congressional representative delivers persuasive speeches on the House floor yet also listens carefully to constituents at public hearings. Effective civic education must involve the development of the ability to listen as part of communication skills.

Service-learning programs that employ appropriate and varied reflection strategies heighten students' communicative abilities. Through reflecting on their service experiences, students are called upon to give an account of themselves and their thoughts in classroom discussions, in oral or artistic presentations, and in their writings (see Battistoni, 1997a: 95–96, for examples from student reflections). In addition, the community service experience itself can teach students to listen to the stories and needs of others. When tutoring, visiting an elderly person, serving overnight in a homeless shelter, or doing an oral history, our students learn, in a tangible way, the art of listening. But once again, as I will argue more forcefully on the pages that follow, for these skills to be most effectively developed as civic skills, time and effort must be spent in structuring both the service experience and that of the classroom to maximize student dialogue and listening opportunities.

It is no small coincidence that the American Communication Association has established a major initiative in civic engagement, or that some of the best examples of integration of communication-oriented community service with civic education goals come out of communications departments. For one example of a communications assignment with explicitly civic dimensions, see Appendix K on page 84.

Public Problem Solving

The other "participation skill" I want to focus upon is the ability to identify and solve public problems. I mention identifying public problems as important because too often community service and service-learning programs overemphasize the service activity, leading students to conclude that their service is both the problem (what service to perform, how to organize it) and the solution (to larger social problems). The infamous example of the student who told her service-learning director that her service experience was such a meaningful experience that she hoped her children would have the opportunity to work in homeless shelters should remind us that service is not an end in itself (Chi, 1999: 227). Only when service leads students to examine the underlying issues beneath their community work to identify problems, and then explore with fellow citizens possible solutions to these public problems, have we done our best to make service an education for citizenship. A former student of mine makes this point clearly, in an excerpt from a written assignment:

> Community service is nothing new to me. I've always done it wholeheartedly and thought of it as something useful and necessary. However, [in this class] I began to realize that helping individuals is only part of the solution. The scope of the problem was wider social problems, economic problems, social neglect and apathy, political neglect, and without addressing these, nothing could fix the problems individuals face...

Service-learning, then, can be a catalyst to the civic skill of public problem solving, when integrated into curricular readings and assignments.

As an example of the kind of curricular assignment that would support public problem solving, I have had students serving at an organization or school identify the "central public problem" that the organization has been developed to respond to. I ask students not only to state the problem, but also to investigate the causes, consequences, and possible responses to the public problem (see Appendix C on page 73). What I have found is not only does a public problem statement/research assignment serve to get students thinking about the larger political and policy dimensions of the service they are doing, but it also enhances the critical thinking and imagination skills discussed on pages 36 to 37. I have seen students come to the jarring realization that their identification of the public problem that the organization is designed to address differs from the organization's own definition of the central problem. Other students have done research that reveals alternative approaches to tackling the problem from those taken by the organization in which they are serving, also something that promotes the kinds of critical civic skills we need to engender in students. I am not alone in thinking this way: the Westheimer and Kahne study cited above found "compelling evidence that when service experiences are combined with rigorous analysis of related social issues, students do develop attitudes, skills, and knowledge necessary to respond in productive ways" (Westheimer & Kahne, 2000). And recently, Campus Compact for New Hampshire sponsored the publication of a fieldguide, titled *Problem Based Service Learning,* connecting service-learning, action research, and the critical civic skill of public problem solving (see Gordon, 2000).

But problem-solving can go beyond the content or assignments in a service-learning class. Service-learning can not only help students *identify* the problems that underlie the need for service, but it can also enhance their ability to solve public problems. In my experience, students have learned public problem solving skills in the context of working together to make their service placement more meaningful and/or more aligned with their abilities and interests. That is, in countless situations, I have witnessed students, working in teams, having to work through problems at their service sites, problems of organization, effective use of their time, or creative programming. For example, students working in an after-school program complaining about their relationships with site staff and their "not being effectively used" had to meet with the program director and develop an alternative structure that would allow them to interact more with program staff and to creatively plan after-school activities of their own for the children. I am certain that this experience in problem solving at their community service site enhanced not only their work that semester, but also their civic capacity. Other students have learned similar lessons about problem solving through "participant observation," i.e., through watching others at their placement sites work together to solve common concerns:

> Service allows you to work closely with people towards a common, respectable goal. When a group works together towards a common good, it inevitably becomes closer, even if the group is diverse. Working at [my service site], I've seen people of all ages, all races, religions and financial status befriend each other and work successfully together...

Once again, for this to happen, both the service activities and the service-learning program need to be organized so that public problem solving will be one of the outcomes. This is best done by organizing students into service "teams"(where collaborative learning pedagogies can be employed), as opposed to individual placements, and by giving students an active role in the design and structure of the school's service-learning program itself (see Barber & Battistoni, 1993; Battistoni, 1996; Wade, 1997).

Civic Judgment

A service-learning program aimed at civic education should also develop students' moral disposition of civic judgment related to their professed values. By civic judgment I mean the ability to use publicly defendable moral standards in application to the actual life and history of a community. The teaching of civic values and their application seems missing in today's university. In a recent essay in *The Atlantic,* for example, David Brooks chronicles the lives of current Ivy League students, whose high levels of personal achievement and politeness are countered by a seeming absence of civic values or deeper moral concerns (Brooks, 2001).

Of course, the language of moral judgment raises red flags in the minds of many, and may not be seen as a desirable skill to develop. In a pluralistic society, the development of students' moral values can be controversial. Discussions of civic values and their application, especially in courses outside of political philosophy, can be uncomfortable for faculty and students alike. How can I as a faculty member venture down this road of moral values without sounding too ideological, even preachy? How can I raise moral questions without causing severe conflicts in the classroom? Well, one mechanism I have used to get students to explore and defend their own civic values—without causing these undesirable side effects—is an exercise asking them to write their own philosophies of service. Although intended as an individual statement of the student's personal values attached to service (hence its attraction to students in service-learning courses), I ask the students to make connections to understandings of community and citizenship. Students, while writing individual philosophies of service, also have the opportunity to share their statements with peers and receive feedback (see Appendix D on page 74).

When tied to assignments like this, you can see how a citizenship-oriented service-learning program can develop capacities for civic judgment. Moreover, the practical experience students gain through their community involvement allows them to set and reset their standards of judgment, and it may cause them to modify their political judgments in reaction to the world they observe and the people with whom they interact:

> I think this class has really opened a lot of people's eyes to what they are like, and what their communities are like. I also think it has made people more aware of the different perspectives we all have. …It is an incredible feeling to be able to see things from a different perspective.

> I learned a lot more about the views which I differ from. And in fact I have changed some of my previous beliefs after reading, hearing, and experiencing the "other side."

These two excerpts help make the case for using community service to develop skills of civic judgment, and even suggest that students emerge from a quality service-learning experience more open and tolerant (see Walt Whitman Center, 1996, for further evidence with respect to religious and racial tolerance).

Civic Imagination and Creativity

But beyond enhancing traditional measures of openness and tolerance, service-learning can encourage the crucial civic competence of imagination. Imagination involves the ability to think creatively about public problems. It has been my experience that civic education—and higher education more generally—tends to privilege the cognitive and analytical almost to the exclusion of the imaginative. Good citizenship, however, requires both capacities.

Civic creativity can be understood in a number of ways. In his "Letter from Birmingham Jail," Martin Luther King, Jr. speaks of nonviolent direct action as a process of "creative tension":

> Nonviolent direct action works to create such a crisis and foster such a tension that a community which has constantly refused to negotiate is forced to confront the issue. It seeks so to *dramatize* the issue that it can no longer be ignored. …Just as Socrates felt that it was necessary to create a tension in the mind so that individuals could rise from the bondage of myths and half-truths to the unfettered realm of *creative* analysis and objective appraisal, so must we see the need for nonviolent gadflies to create the kind of tension in society that will help men rise from the dark depths of prejudice and racism to the majestic heights of understanding and brotherhood.

> —Martin Luther King, Jr. 1999: 397, emphasis added

King saw the creativity and dramatic flair involved in nonviolent civil disobedience as pivotal to the process of social change and growth. In a similar vein, Craig Rimmerman's discussion of the unconventional politics of the "new citizenship" highlights the creativity and artistic capacities involved in the activities of groups like ACT UP, Earth First!, and Operation Rescue (Rimmerman, 1997). But in my way of thinking, civic creativity involves the use of imaginative capacities to achieve anything of public value.

There are two dimensions to civic imagination, the personal and the political. In *The Imaginary Domain*, Drucilla Cornell outlines the imagination's personal impact, by making important connections between an individual's self-image and full personhood. In the context of discussing legal restrictions on abortion, pornography, and sexual harassment, Cornell contends that "the project of becoming a person is dependent on the psychic space of the imagination," i.e., on the individual's ability to imagine "who one is and who one seeks to become" unhindered by the potentially degrading effects of narrow public depictions (particularly sexual and gender images). For Cornell, an individual can only be free to the extent that she has the space to develop and renew her imagination (Cornell, 1995). Beyond the individual self, democratic necessities like compassion and tolerance require imagination, the capacity to imagine oneself in the place of others who face vastly different circumstances, and ultimately, to work together with them to achieve common purposes. Imagination also must be present if we are to maintain the ability to project and embrace a collective vision for the future, as it implies the capacity to think about ourselves and our community in ways not tied to the past; to "dream things that never were and ask, 'Why not?'" as George Bernard Shaw put it (cited in Battistoni, 1991: 13).

Students' imaginative abilities can be enhanced through service-learning, by enlarging their sense of who they are and enabling them to use their imagination to join together in working toward a common goal with people who have different backgrounds, values, and life stories. Especially when conducted through curricula in the visual or performing arts, a community-based service experience can act as a catalyst for the development of this kind of capacity. A number of great examples exist. The Imagining America Project based at the University of Michigan—a "national consortium of colleges, universities, and cultural institutions dedicated to supporting the civic work of university artists, humanists, and designers"—is one of these (see http://www.ia.umich.edu/ for details of the project). Excellent course-based models for integrating service, civic values, and the performing arts can be found in the Women's Studies and Psychology volumes of the AAHE Series on Service-Learning in the Disciplines (see Backman, 2000; Carlebach & Singer, 1998; respectively). And finally, I include a sample course assignment in Appendix E (see page 75) that integrates community-based work in the dramatic arts with civic purposes.

Collective Action

Democratic citizenship certainly involves cognitive, communicative, and problem-solving skills. But it is also about taking action, both individually and together with members of one's community. Alexis de Tocqueville may have laid out most clearly the argument for taking collective action in community-based organizations as essential to maintaining democratic institutions and to educating people for citizenship. He argued that in democracies "all the citizens are independent and feeble; they can do hardly anything by themselves, and none of them can oblige [others] to lend their assistance. They all therefore become powerless if they do not learn voluntarily to help one another." Participation in civic associations educates people to overcome this powerlessness and isolation, since through this participation members of associations learn "the art of pursuing in common the object of their common desires" and of "proposing a common object for the exertions of a great many and inducing them voluntarily to pursue it" (Tocqueville, 1945: 115). More recently, Robert Putnam (1995, 2000) has echoed Tocqueville's argument, lamenting the decline in voluntary associations and the subsequent loss of "social capital," the foundation of our democracy.

Meta Mendel-Reyes defines the central skill involved here: "To take collective action, the members of a community need to figure out ways to work together while acknowledging their differences, one of the most difficult lessons to learn in the classroom as well as in politics" (Mendel-Reyes, 1998). Service-learning courses can produce this result, especially when they integrate assignments designed to translate service into collective public action (see Walker, 2000, and Appendix F on page 76 for an example from her service-learning course).

Community/Coalition Building

Before being able to take collective action, citizens need to be able to work together across their differences to create the very collective capable of taking action on matters of common concern. For some, this capacity is called community building, and has a long tradition in political theory and civic education (see, for example, Mendel-Reyes, 1998: 37). But I prefer the language of coalition or alliance building, as it seems more fitting to citizenship in a diverse, democratic society. Too often when using the language of community building, we fall into habits of seeking a comfortable consensus, something that reminds us of the community of home and family. Bernice Johnson Reagon reminds us, however, that there is a vast difference between "home" and "coalition," between family and civic engagement. While we may like to build communities—rooms of sameness and comfort—these exclusive homes are often barred to designated others, and ultimately, "there is no chance you can survive by staying inside the barred room" (Reagon, 1998). Coalition or alliance building acknowledges that we begin with diverse identities and interests, but that we must find commonality in order to address matters of mutual concern. It requires citizens, in the words of Shane Phelan, "to build a ground together instead of finding one and inviting others to sit on it" (Phelan, 1994: 158).

Whether we call it community or coalition building, service-learning can also teach this critical civic capacity, as it often requires students to come together across a variety of differences. This skill can be enhanced in service-learning courses where students are placed in "teams" at community-based organizations, working on common projects, rather than being placed individually. But like many of the other skills, coalition building does not happen automatically from a service experience. I have found success using a "coalition building exercise," which can be adapted for the subject matter of different service-learning classes (see Appendix G on page 78).

Organizational Analysis

The final civic skill that deserves mention is what I will call organizational analysis. We know from all the research that college-age students have strong antipathies toward politics, traditionally understood. But in addition to being apolitical, especially in their orientation to service, I have found that the students I work with through service-learning programs also tend to be anti-institutional. My students view service as a direct, and therefore preferable, form of intervention into a problem or situation. They are not inclined to consider the organizational structures or imperatives (and therefore, the power structures) within which their service necessarily takes place. In general, I have found students often to be initially oblivious to the organizational structure or staffing at their service placement, preferring to "plunge in" to their service experience. In being oriented to their service work, students are not always offered a detailed picture of the mission, goals, or history of the organization, let alone the areas of public policy that might affect its work. Rarely have I found students to inquire without prodding about the organization's budget or efforts at fundraising, and what this tells us about its work. My own findings track consistently with the authors of *The Good Society,* who argue that though "we live through institutions," Americans fear and have trouble understanding organizational structures (Bellah, et al., 1992: 3–18). And yet, without considering the organizational "text" and "context" of their service work, our students will certainly be less effective servants, let alone citizens (see Hildreth, 2000; Lakey, et al., 1995).

To be effective as paid workers, volunteers, or citizens, students need to be able to understand the settings in which they operate. This means that they need to be able to analyze a budget, and to map the interests and power relationships of the people within the institutions that directly or indirectly affect their work. Students' participation in community-based organizations should be accompanied by educational efforts aimed at "thickening those bonds of connectedness" formed by such participation with adults in civic associations (Campbell, 2000). For example, students doing service work in a community-based organization can be given academic assignments that require them to learn more about the organization's operation and interactions with the community and with government. They can be asked to gather and dissect the budget, organizational chart, and mission of the organization, to interview key staff and board members, or to engage in "power mapping" exercises. (See Appendix H on page 79 for a sample assignment in organizational analysis.) In this way, a service-learning experience can foster organizational analysis skills, and can deepen a student's understanding of the role of civic or not-for-profit organizations in American public life more generally.

chapter six

What Is Good Citizenship?
STUDENT VOICES

> Each age, it is found, must write its own books; or rather, each generation for the next succeeding. The books of an older period will not fit this.
>
> —Ralph Waldo Emerson

Over the past decade, higher education has done plenty of hand wringing over its ineffectiveness in moving students to active democratic citizenship. A number of solutions have been proposed, including the use of service-learning tied to various curricula with a civic engagement emphasis. I have tried to offer a variety of conceptual frameworks and possible skill-based foundations for faculty in any discipline to pursue this strategy.

But in all of this effort, little has been done to actually listen to this generation of college students and how *they* frame the question of civic engagement. Two notable exceptions exist: the 1993 Kettering Foundation report "College Students Talk Politics," and a recent Wingspread Student Summit on Civic Engagement sponsored by Campus Compact held in March 2001. Over the same decade, I have sought to chronicle the wide variety of civic attitudes and perspectives held by students I have taught on three different urban campuses. From the written reflections of students in service-learning courses, I have gleaned powerful statements of civic purpose, albeit framed in different terms than either national studies of youth disengagement or political theories of civic education might capture. With the help of these three sources, let me reframe the question, What is good citizenship?

Re-Framing Political Knowledge:
Citizenship as Better Knowledge of Communities And Their Concerns

Some of the evidence about youth civic disengagement centers on lack of interest in or knowledge about politics and government. But if we listen to young people we get a different picture than that of political ignorance. Those scholars who talk about the importance of acquiring political knowledge have a fairly traditional understanding of what constitutes knowledge. To them, a good civic education means assimilating political information, like the provisions of the Bill of Rights, the names and party affiliations of congressional representatives, and the answer to the perennial question of "how a bill becomes a law" (see Delli Carpini & Keeter, 1996, for detailed lists). Our students, however, understand the knowledge question very differently. At Wingspread, students involved in community service work talked about their engagement as a way of gaining knowledge about the larger community. Our colleges and universities are often disconnected, intentionally in many cases, from the neighborhoods of which they are immediately a part. For students attending urban institutions, especially non-commuters, the "town-gown" disconnect is quite clear, as these representative observations from Rutgers University students at the beginning of their service-learning class indicate:

> In between [campuses] lies a more harsh neighborhood of New Brunswick. Although the students ride through this area daily to and from [the campuses]...it may as well be on another planet. The University community barely acknowledges the existence of this area, as well as many others in New Brunswick, I'm sure. It's very sad, but I am as guilty as anyone. When riding that route I barely give this area a thought. It never occurs to me that I live two minutes from this area—and yet I think of this place as another world.

> [Our] school is located in the city of New Brunswick but there is little connection between the two. If community includes geographic area then the school should be interacting with the city but unfortunately it doesn't. In fact, most students are afraid of any citizen of New Brunswick who walks by and every girl seems to be carrying mace. Crime is a definite fear but it inhibits Rutgers students from talking and connecting to New Brunswick people especially since there seems to be an economic distinction.

I have found that one of the more important outcomes of my service-learning courses for students who are not local residents is that they get to know the metropolitan area and its citizens in a way they would never have known without service-learning. Two different seniors reported that, for the first time in their college careers, they were able to "get to know [their] neighbors in the larger community." Another student wrote that his experiences made him comfortable walking, jogging, and shopping in and around housing projects that bordered the campus, greeting people he was working with on site, putting a lie to the message of the campus orientation program: "don't leave the campus." The written reflections of three students add to this dimension of learning about citizenship:

> When I went on the neighborhood walk during the first week of class, I remember thinking that many of the houses were somewhat run down and they reminded me a lot of the low-income housing projects that were in my town. I look back on that experience and think how wrong I was. Now that I've been in this service-learning class, I go into those same neighborhoods many times during the week to go to the store and meet many of the people who live in the neighborhood. For me it all relates back to what Dr. King said, that you have to look past the religion or color of the person in order to see the true person.

> I think I truly learned more clearly to understand the development of the neighborhood and its present day condition. I have never learned so much history packed into one neighborhood. I was glad to have had the opportunity to "walk through history" and gain an appreciation of what there is around me at [the college]. I now do not see it as a "bad section" neighborhood but rather a piece of history that should have been preserved and maintained so that it does not lose its historical environment.

For those students who come from the surrounding metropolitan communities, service-learning can give them a better knowledge of the community with which they identify but of which they are not nearly as knowledgeable as they originally thought. One Salvadoran student I taught wrote that the service-learning course she took made her more aware of her own community: "Even though I'm from Providence, I learned I didn't know the community as well as I thought I did, especially the needs of racial and ethnic minorities other than my own." An African-American woman at Rutgers testified powerfully about how, though she was from an urban area and was working with younger African-American students in a "girl's club rap session" as part of an after-school program, she was unaware until she participated in service of the differences these girls' generation faced from the ones she did, especially with respect to issues around violence and sexuality:

> Many of the girls...have brought up the topic of sex. They come in with many questions and beliefs, misconstrued at times...I tried to correct their misunderstandings, to teach them to respect themselves and others,...to teach them self-reliance and self-sufficiency, but found myself ineffective because my own situation as a teenager was so different from that of these girls....I feel I owe it to my race and my culture to reach out and try to help the children of the future become better able to survive in this world, and now I know better what young African-American girls face in the world.

Students, whether from different places or backgrounds, or from the local community, see themselves as ignorant of the complex public problems that create the need for the service they do. From the students' perspective, service *is* a form of political knowledge, as it teaches them about the real-life problems faced by the community with which they work. James Carignan's discussion of the model service-learning program at Bates College echoes my own (see Carignan, 1998: 40–57).

Students also seem conscious of specific issues rather than the political system as a whole. They see their service work as a way of concretely understanding the personal dimensions of social and public policy issues. This perspective was clear in the Kettering study, where students reported the "need to know about specific issues" (Harwood Group, 1993: 4), but also the difficulty of being informed due to the way issues are presented by the national/popular media.

For faculty wishing to draw students out from their specific service to understand underlying public issues, the implications seem clear. We need to structure some of our readings and assignments around the work that our students are doing, to maximize connections to the acquisition of this kind of political knowledge. For example, in my introductory service-learning courses, I have started to assign different readings to groups of students doing work involving different issues. I ask each group to make presentations, including written presentations, that combine their service experiences with the outside reading about the issue in question (see Appendix I for an example of this approach). As another example, two faculty at California State University, Fresno—one from mathematics and one from communications—designed an "issue oriented multidisciplinary service-learning course focused on the 2000 Census (see Heffernan, 2001: 114–117). A "public issues" approach to service-learning can be a particularly powerful vehicle for faculty in professional or pre-professional academic programs, where students can be connected through their service to public issues of central concern to the profession.

Re-Framing the Common Good: Identity, Diversity, and "Pluralistic Citizenship"

Another problem with the way we frame the question of civic education has been that while we proclaim the need to prepare citizens for the "hard work" of finding common ground in a diverse democracy, we often emphasize community over diversity. For this generation of college students, however, diversity may be the overarching priority. The students at Wingspread gave powerful testimony to the hard work involved in embracing diversity and widening inclusion on their campuses and in their communities. For today's students working through diversity to achieve community involves not only confronting "isms" and dealing with issues of race, class, gender, and sexuality. Students deeply engaged in community work also experience injustices based on religion, language, culture, age, disability, and geography. The students interviewed for the Kettering report emphasized diversity of perspective as well. "Students say that it is important to understand the full range of perspectives on issues if political discussions are to be productive" (Harwood Group, 1993: 23). For these students, the most important civic skills were expressed as "the ability to keep an open mind, to stand in another person's shoes, to change, and to make decisions with others" who do not share your own background or perspective (Harwood Group, 1993: vii).

Community service can be a powerful vehicle for exploring questions concerning one's place as a citizen in a multicultural democracy. I have written elsewhere about the powerful insights connecting democracy and diversity that can come in a curriculum incorporating community service involvement (Battistoni, 1995). Listen to the words of a variety of students that reveal the possibility of learning about citizenship in a pluralistic society through service-learning:

> I do not come from a diverse background. My contacts and friendships have always been with people very similar to myself. [M]y service is helping me become a more diverse person...[by] coming into contact with people of cultures different than my own.

> My images of race come from the media and movies mainly—unfortunately. Dealing with different races [through community service] provides alternative images of other races than what is fed to us on the news or in movies. At [my service site] I am able to interact with all different races who are positive people/role models for the community. Probably being involved in service could improve race relations in the general public. Those being helped and those who help get alternate images of different races. Not to say that all students [at my site] are minorities or all tutors, teachers, volunteers are white: it is just the opposite—all races occupy all roles and provide an alternative to classification and stereotyping.

> The structure of this course...has helped me to think. [D]ifference and racism...are issues very close to me, and yet at times so distant. [A]s a student of Indian origin, I have often been at the receiving end of racial prejudice. Despite this fact, I am not too knowledgeable on this issue, for in order to know an issue well, one has to be able to discuss both sides of it. I often treat it as a closed issue, seeing myself as a victim and the rest of American society as oppressive. I see this problem amplified several times in my father and his Indian friends. I listen to the way that my father and other adult friends talk about such issues. The unfortunate thing is that such talk often influences my thinking and results in a polarization of myself into my private and public selves. In public I may at times hide my particular biases, in order to appease the other ethnic groups. But then in private, I see myself often as trying to justify my biases through my friends, family, and the Indian community. Why do I have this problem? Because I don't think about the issue in depth. I recognize the issues like prejudice and racism in con-

versations and while watching TV. But I do not pick apart these issues often. I store them away in the cobwebs of my brain. So, I feel that by making me reflect deeply on such issues through class discussion, various readings and journals, and in my community service, where I work with African-American and Hispanic youth corps members with backgrounds and lifestyles very different from my own, it has helped me to some extent in unifying my two selves.

As you can see from this last quote, the images of diversity and difference that emerge in service-learning curricula are not simple or unproblematic. For example, for students of color or those whose background or status has often placed them in an "oppressed minority" status, community experiences can be the source of deep conflict. I have worked with a number of African-American students for whom the language of citizenship connected to service had great power, but it was understood first as "cultural citizenship," a way of explaining how and why "I can contribute or give something back to *my* community." It also prompted them to challenge white students doing work in communities of color, and to make observations about the segregation of students on campus, especially in the dining halls.

For those of us interested in pursuing the connections between citizenship and diversity, we must not diminish the difficult conflicts that may emerge, for both teacher and students. One African-American student whose family had once received public assistance and who was in college on full financial aid was challenged as one of the privileged elite by the high school dropouts with whom he was working at his service site. A Korean woman had to courageously deal with the racism of her family as they tried to forbid her from even participating in a service-learning class. A Latino student spoke eloquently, both in class and in this journal entry, about how his service work brought his own personal story to light:

> I am a Hispanic minority. [M]y parents worked hard and made enough money for us to live comfortably in an upper middle class neighborhood. My memories of living in an urban neighborhood in an apartment building are so vague in my mind they seem as almost a movie I watched years ago. I feel distanced from the experience. Working at [my service site] brought back these old experiences and made them a reality. It did occur to me it was not all a bad dream. I escaped in this sense I am truly a minority because the majority of these people do not escape. It's a perpetual cycle of degradation.

And a gay student was forced to confront and overcome the homophobia of minority children in an urban after-school enrichment program:

> I wear two earrings in my left ear, and one in my right ear. In the first 15 minutes I had a swarm of kids around me asking me why I had earrings in both ears, because only "gays" did that. They said I looked like a girl and actually demanded that I remove two of the three earrings. First, I am gay, and it made me feel very uncomfortable having that be an issue in my first 15 minutes on the job. I felt awkward. Also the kids threw the word "faggot" around like it was nothing. This was very hurtful for me, but I swallowed it, removed the earrings and pressed on. It was not how I anticipated the start of my volunteer work. It got better though. The spirit, enthusiasm, and openness of the kids swept me away. I could not believe how friendly and forward they were, virtually fighting over me to check their homework. It was really great.

As you can imagine, these kinds of community-based experiences are both powerful and difficult to process. They offer "teachable moments" for faculty and can serve to render the concepts of "diversity" and "citizenship" themselves much more complex than at first glance. (For further discussion, with detailed examples from students engaged in service-learning, see Dunlap, 2000.)

On the connections between civic engagement and diversity, we have cause for celebration, not only from my report from the Wingspread Student Summit, but from the work of educational organizations. Through efforts like the AACU's Democracy, Diversity, and Liberal Learning project, faculty have come to see how their own discipline-based courses—including those involving service-learning—might be tied to other campus initiatives around diversity and multiculturalism (see Knefelkamp and Schneider, 1997). Most recently, Sylvia Hurtado at the University of Michigan is leading a research project, *Preparing College Students for a Diverse Democracy*, aimed at connecting programmatic and curricular initiatives at ten universities to "cognitive, social, and democratic skills" necessary for living in a diverse democracy (described in Schneider, 2001).

Re-Framing Political Participation: Democratizing the Campus and Classroom

Institutions of higher learning certainly affect what students know about politics. Sometimes they learn what politics is in class. Most of the time they learn politics from the way it is practiced on campus.

—David Mathews, "Introduction," in Harwood Group, 1993: xi

Usually, my classes consist of reading the text then being lectured on the material the next day. Although I do learn from this I don't feel involved or integrated with the class and material we are covering. So, this course was a new experience for me. In this course I get the chance to express my views and experiences to the rest of the class. I also hear my classmates' opinions and views on certain topics. I enjoy this because I often don't talk to my peers about social prejudices, community service or democracy even though these are big concerns of modern times. By hearing other college students' beliefs on these topics it helps me understand my own feelings and come to terms with them. By having a discussion type of format...it also forces me to relate the topic we are covering to my own life and experiences. Many times I've thought of incidents I haven't thought of in years and this has helped me understand myself and the subject more.

So far, my discussion of the different perspectives on democratic citizenship that emerge from students engaged in education-based community service has focused on the content of civic lessons learned. But students in both the Kettering report and the Wingspread Student Summit argued that democratic processes, particularly pedagogical processes, are equally important. When the classroom is itself a democratic community, where equal participation and voice is invited and expected, students and faculty gain a better sense of the civic meaning of group responsibility, reciprocity, interdependence, and intercultural cooperation (or conflict!). Students in my service-learning classes have commented on the impact created by more democratic classroom interaction:

[The classroom] format is extremely beneficial to each of us because we are encouraged to express our thoughts, opinions, and beliefs as a group. It helps us to create a community within the classroom. We all come together as a unit responding to all of the issues we face relating to community.

[D]emocracy is key in understanding the work that is performed by the participants of [service-learning] classes....The class itself is considered a small group community whose goals it is to bring about a sense of friendship and trust within its participants. In my [service-learning course] I became directly involved with my classmates in open discussions on past experiences in different styles of community. This free class structure is conducive to interactive learning with my peers. For a semester I was involved in class discussions which tended to continue outside of the classroom. This issues which are discussed are everyday occurrences which all who serve encounter. In one particular instance, my service group was experiencing difficulties with the staff at our service site. The class dynamic, which is relaxed and non-judgmental, changed to accommodate the needs of my small group to discuss the difficulties and work at a solution....As in a functioning community, all members came together to help sort out a problem and offer varied views on an approach. This openness with class members provides for a friendly environment [and] encourages the building of class community.

As with almost everything else, the creation of a democratic classroom is not an automatic consequence of service-learning. Too often, even the service-learning classroom mirrors the hierarchy of what has alternately been called the "vertical cultural transmission model" (Mead, 1958), the "static, cold-storage ideal of knowledge" (Dewey, 1916: 158–9), and the "banking concept of education" (Freire, 1970). Although it is a pedagogical practice that has been condemned by democratic educators throughout the twentieth century, it has remarkable resilience, and even fits well with certain notions of educational reform and assessment, especially at the K-12 level. To create a democratic classroom involves much greater time and effort in coordinating and structuring activities and class discussions, and much more attention to "process," than does a "traditional" classroom. Additionally, when successful, a democratic service-learning class may cause students cognitive dissonance, especially if a democratic pedagogy conflicts with the school's institutional or academic culture. But if we in service-learning are to regard ourselves as "progressive educators," defined by Paulo Freire as those who "favor the autonomy of the students" (Freire, 1998: 21), then we must give greater attention to democratic practices in the classroom and on our campuses, no matter what the cognitive or political dissonance our students may experience. (For an extensive discussion of the opportunities and challenges of a more democratic pedagogy, see Battistoni, 2000.)

Re-Imagining Political Change: Thinking Locally, Acting Globally
On one question, the students I work with, the Wingspread Student Summit participants, and the Kettering report's student focus groups all agree with the characterizations of them in national surveys as disengaged. Students have rejected national politics as an arena in which to achieve the changes they seek. On the one hand, students do not see national politics as a place where they can make a difference: "Students do not believe their voice is being heard. If we knew that we were being heard, we'd make more of an effort to do things" (Harwood Group, 1993: 29). On the other hand, students—especially those engaged in community service—see the citizens they have come to care about being closed out from the political process. In fact, a recurrent theme at the Wingspread

Student Summit on Civic Engagement was that politics needed to be responsive to those currently shut out from the process. This sentiment has also arisen in my student's reflections, as evidenced by this Providence College student from fall 2000:

> I find it ever so ironic that the government argues that people are too dependant on public assistance, preaching for less federal intervention, but yet complain about people's lack of interest in politics. It is a mutual relationship in many ways, not a give or a take exclusively. Why be interested in a system that is fundamentally not the least bit interested in you? This may seem contrary to Kennedy's advice to ask what we could do for our government, but it is not. I simply find it very difficult to ask someone who was forgotten, looked over, and deserted in their suffering to run to the voting booths to promote a candidate that never looked twice. My general philosophy is that I want to be as aware as possible so that the fairly unrepresentative representatives in Washington, D.C. can pull as little wool as possible over my eyes. Also, I feel that as a minority woman, I cannot risk being uninformed or ignorant, and I must be able to form concrete, articulate opinions about such issues. There is some truth in the belief that for every step they take, I must make two.

Many students seek a politics that includes everyone affected by decisions at the table, including young people. National politics is seen as being exclusionary, and therefore undesirable.

As a result, students who may be disengaged from national politics nonetheless see themselves as actively engaged at the local level. One student interviewed in the Panetta Institute survey contended that volunteer service was "an influence in a more immediate way, whereas in politics it's a little slower in getting to the individual" (Panetta Institute, 2000). A recent student of mine echoed this sentiment, claiming additionally that local community service was actually a way of taking responsibilities away from the federal government and placing them in the hands of more personal institutions:

> By volunteering in your community you are performing a good service because you are caring for the people around you. When they receive aid from individuals that are concerned as opposed to receiving a check from a big impersonal corporation the effect is more positive. A loving and caring sentiment is sent through the town. As a young adult of the United States, I feel that service is a huge part of my citizenship. Serving makes me feel as if I am helping to improve society's conditions. The concept of service is more tangible than concepts such as voting, paying taxes, and keeping the peace. I feel more involved emotionally and physically with a community when completing a task such as service.

At Wingspread, a number of students made a different connection between disengagement from national politics and active engagement in local service. When national public policies have the effect of throwing citizens into the river, they argued, the service that pulls one's neighbor out is a political act, albeit not one that can be measured through traditional indicators like voting.

Today's students also seem to be energized by global concerns, understanding that in a complex democratic society and an increasingly globalized economy the targets for public action are multiple, requiring multiple strategies. One student at the Wingspread Student Summit put it this way:

We embrace our identities, we are a multi-tendency and cross-cultural group of citizens untangling problems on a local level that, for the first time in history, are inseparable from the global critique. We live in an age of global economy and global politics, of which no clear, singular "enemies" exist.

From protests against the World Trade Organization to work on campuses to fight against sweatshop labor, especially in the manufacture of items with school logos and emblems, many students today are finding meaning in movements for global change. Whatever the ultimate target for their actions, we should concede that students engaged in "service" may actually be experimenting with ways to "think locally and learn to act with an impact on the larger world" (Boyte, 1999: 177).

What can faculty take away from these student voices, some of whom contradict national findings about youth civic disengagement? The most important thing I take away is the imperative that we make room in our practices and in our curriculum for a conversation where students name for themselves what it is they are doing and its connection to community, citizenship, and democratic politics (see Morton & Battistoni, 1995). In my experience, this means beginning with students' motivations, language, and philosophies around service, all of which may be private or apolitical, and using politically-oriented texts or materials, to determine whether a more civic or public language resonates with their aspirations (see Battistoni, 1997a; Walker, 2000). In this sense, our campuses and courses need to be a resource to help this generation of students find political answers for themselves, knowing with Jefferson and Emerson that each generation makes its own constitution and writes its own books. Related to this, we need to pay greater attention to the role students can play in the design and management of our campus service-learning programs in general. Students should play an active role in planning the program and serve as leaders in it not only because students have good ideas and can recruit and organize other students, but also because active participation in service-learning can help students learn the lessons of democracy. (For a more extensive argument, see Battistoni, 1996.)

Additionally, in revising our academic programs to take account of civic engagement goals, we need to ask how our students actually encounter our curriculum. Do students experience our courses as majors, minors, or as part of the core/general education requirements of the college? Do they typically take one course in our department/program or is service-learning incorporated as part of a developmental, laddered curriculum? Do we work with graduate students, those coming to us for pre-professional mentoring, or those seeking to hone their research skills? How important is the pedagogy of our courses to our students' experiences? What about departmentally based clubs, honor societies, or other extra-curricular opportunities we offer? Do we need to consider the specific characteristics of the students at our institution—a significant percentage of international students, non-traditional students juggling multiple responsibilities, or commuter as opposed to residential students—in designing our service-learning courses? Answers to all of these questions vary, but they certainly should shape the strategies by which we implement service-learning with civic engagement as an ultimate aim.

chapter seven

Being Attentive to the Civic Dimensions of Service-Learning

I have tried to make a case for service-learning as a vehicle to civic education across the disciplines. Service-learning is a powerful pedagogy based in the recognition that "democracy is a learned activity and that active participation in the life of a community is a bridge to citizenship" (Saltmarsh & Hollander, 2000). A properly designed service experience can be a civically transformative one because students are immersed in a community setting, potentially working with an organization or a school on an issue of public dimensions, working with people coming from different backgrounds or with different interests in the issue. It offers, in a way that classroom or traditional texts cannot, a tangible context for exploring and understanding the very issues of public concern that give rise to the needs for community service. As mentioned earlier, however, a review of the literature strongly suggests that the connection between service and civic engagement is not automatic. So the question remains, how do we create *optimal conditions* under which service-learning can translate into civic learning?

Before looking at strategies for civic engagement, we need to acknowledge that there are a number of specific challenges to doing this work, beyond those posed by our students discussed at the end of the last chapter. In our work over the past two years with the Campus Compact Intermediate Institute for Engaged Departments, my colleagues Sherril Gelmon and Jon Wergin and I have heard faculty and community partners identify a number of departmental and community-based barriers to civic engagement. Some of the most pertinent are included in figure three on the following page.

FIGURE 3:

Barriers to Civic Engagement in Higher Education

Departmental/Pedagogical Barriers

- Time and resources for implementation; engagement is seen as an "add-on"

- Inequitable workloads, compensation for part-time or pre-tenure faculty, for whom civic engagement is an imposition

- Lack of tangible support, or at the very least, mixed messages from academic leadership

- Hostility/resistance from influential faculty

- Adding to an already-full course; fear of a loss of disciplinary content when doing community-based engagement

- Getting from concrete experience to abstract concepts and theories

- Little to no sense of collective responsibility; courses seen as "proprietary" by individuals

- Student/faculty ratios that are not conducive to civic engagement

- Reward system, especially promotion and tenure guidelines, not supportive

Community Barriers

- Community partners' time; extra work of service-learning for citizens already overburdened

- Concerns that students are not adequately prepared for community work; students will have stereotypes cultivated by experience

- Addressing both community and academic goals with the same experience

- Community partners' buy-in of faculty scholarship interests; biases of community professionals toward democratic engagement

- Logistics: transportation to sites, scheduling, liability risks

These challenges acknowledged, based on my work with students at three different campuses over the past twelve years, I can venture tentative conclusions about what the elements of curriculum quality might be, if civic engagement is one of our desired outcomes. Listening to the voices and concerns of students in ways suggested in chapter 6 is certainly one element of program quality. But I can think of three other program quality factors, drawing upon the work of Janet Eyler and Dwight Giles (1999: 32–34). In discussing the impact of service-learning on personal and interpersonal outcomes related to "diversity," they found three program quality factors within service-learning that enhanced student learning: 1) placement quality ("the quality of the actual service experience"); 2) application and reflection (application is defined as "the extent to which the academic study is related to the nature of the service experience"; reflection as "explicit attempts to consider subject matter in the light of experience"); and 3) community voice (the extent to which the community is involved in defining service needs and in contributing to the desired student learning outcomes). I believe these factors can be extrapolated for faculty concerned about enhancing civic learning outcomes. (For a similar argument applied to K-12 service-learning, see Battistoni, 2000.) In general, it may be useful, in thinking about "quality service-learning," to regard the community service connected to any politically oriented learning as one of the central "texts." (For a good definition of "service as text," see Morton, 1996.)

Placement Quality

To regard the community service experience as "text" means that the service placement needs to be pre-examined to make sure it can be "mined" for civic or political themes. If we seek democratic civic learning outcomes, not just any service experience will do. As with any text, faculty should choose the kind of service attached to a political science course intentionally, with a view to enhancing the political content of the course. Opportunities for students to work in campaigns and elections (like my American Government course example discussed earlier) or with political parties, with public agencies, or in community organizing or community development might be the most conducive to drawing forth civic lessons from students. But there are also examples where service that is not directly "political" can offer rich civic learning opportunities. (For specific examples, see Heffernan, 2001, especially chapter four: "Civic Bridges.") Assignments such as those included in the appendices offer ideas on how to transform what may seem to be nonpolitical community service into a vehicle for civic engagement. That brings us to the critical role played by application and reflection.

Application and Reflection

Beyond the selection of "politically rich" community-based service experiences, faculty should structure their courses more consciously, to allow for structured opportunities for students to critically reflect upon the political aspects of the text that is their service work, as well as the civic nature of the other, written texts. Additionally, faculty using a community-based experience as a "text" need to be familiar with the lived service text, as they would any written text, which calls for greater engagement in the community partnership than we typically see in service-learning, at least understanding the dimensions and complexities of students' service, so as to be able to ask the right (i.e., civically oriented) questions in class or in written assignments (see appendices for examples). This can be accomplished through lectures, assignments, simulations, service-site group presentations, and class discussions.

But the most important component is critical reflection. For service-learning to work optimally as a vehicle for civic education, students need to be pushed to dig deeper in their thinking/reflection on the service experience, beyond how they feel or what they are doing or the charitable motivations behind what they're doing to the "civic" or "public" dimensions of their work. This means that they need to be willing to critically examine their experience as they would any other text in a classroom setting. This is something that can be difficult for students, many of whom want to do service to avoid critically analyzing or reflecting, particularly in terms of political awareness or democratic civic practice. They want to act, to make an immediate difference. Fighting this inclination is important, because as I mentioned above, in addition to being primarily apolitical in their orientation to service, young people also tend to be anti-institutional. Some of the questions included in Appendix B may begin to challenge students to think in more civic ways.

Community Voice

Eyler and Giles emphasize the importance of establishing service projects that meet "community-identified needs," and I would agree that this is one element in quality service-learning. To continue the metaphor, the community-based experience is not a text faculty members choose by themselves. But paying attention to community-identified needs is not enough. Too often service-learning programs make sure the community's need is articulated in setting up the service activity, but they basically treat the organization as a "placement site," rather than as a real partner in education. To create a partnership between campus and community means that both sides need to "re-imagine themselves as members of the same community, each with resources to offer, the right to make claims on the other, and a stake that causes them to work out differences" (Morton, 1997: 11). This begs the question: Does the campus as a whole act as a good *institutional* citizen in the larger community? Does it approach the community as a "partner in education" rather than a set of clients to be served? Partnership underscores mutual interdependence and helps create an understanding of community—not as those with problems but as the group to which we all belong.

At the very least, the university and community partners must exhibit a commitment to collaborate together to provide proper orientation to both the community and the specific organization with which students are working, so that students see the *civic* value in what they are doing. Additionally, faculty need to share their desired learning outcomes with community partners, and invite staff from community-based organizations to play a teaching and evaluation role, either at the site or in the classroom. At Providence College, for example, community partners have played a significant role in strategic planning and curriculum development. We have also created a mechanism for community partners to serve as paid "Community Advisors" to individual courses, with a co-teaching role negotiated with the faculty member assigned to the course. This kind of commitment on the part of community partners is not an easy thing to accomplish, as many have neither the time nor the interest to serve as "co-civic educators." But if service-learning is indeed reciprocal, we have to hold all constituents—including community-based ones—accountable to the mutual interests in long-term collaboration. (For more details on Campus/Community Partnerships, see Campus Compact, 2000.)

Beyond the collaboration between individual faculty members and community partners, campuses can take a number of steps to enhance community voice, both in their service-learning programs and in the institution as a whole. One typical starting point is the creation of advisory committees with significant representation from the community. At Indiana University-Purdue University Indianapolis, for example, community partners have served on a number of different advisory committees to their service-learning program, providing important guidance and feedback, engaging in joint strategic planning, and generally fostering dialogue between the campus and community around items of mutual interest. At Stanford, Penn, and other campuses where participatory action research is practiced (as mentioned earlier) community partners are intimately involved in identifying the research projects that would best serve their needs and goals.

More ambitious efforts at campus-community partnership involve sharing resources. Some campuses have found ways to share space, even investing in shared-use buildings, on or off campus. Other campuses have found ways to extend resources to their neighboring communities in the form of purchasing and hiring policies that favor local residents and businesses. Yet others have made significant investments in the form of direct financial contributions to support housing and economic development in neighborhoods that abut the campus. (For specific examples of these more ambitious initiatives to tangibly improve community voice, see Hollander, et al., 2001.)

Concluding Thoughts

Service-learning can be a particularly effective method of civic education, if we pay close attention to the democratic political outcomes we seek in the design of our programs, curriculum, and pedagogy. "Paying attention" in the specific ways I'm suggesting may seem like a lot to ask of all involved. At the very least, it means paying attention to two critical conditions. The first is my plea to incorporate a diversity of perspectives about what it means to be a "democratic citizen." Narrow or rhetorical definitions of service and citizenship are inadequate to the task of inviting into a public dialogue and public life the people, especially young people, who have walked away. In our thinking about the relationship between the individual self and the community we need to draw upon all perspectives, including those of students themselves. I have offered some ideas about defining civic engagement in a way that might work for you, given your particular disciplinary or institutional context. And we must look closely at the kinds of skills young people need for effective citizenship, some of which I've suggested above, and the connection of these skills to service-learning content and pedagogy. All of this argues in addition for new ways to evaluate or measure the "civic impact" of participation in service-learning.

Secondly, however, we must keep in mind my earlier point that service alone does not automatically lead to engaged citizenship; only if we consciously construct our courses with the education of democratic citizens (broadly understood) in mind can service-learning be one of the vehicles by which we reinvigorate our rapidly deteriorating public life. I have attempted here to make suggestions about how we might rethink our practices in line with outcomes focused on civic engagement. These suggestions about "optimal conditions" may be difficult to achieve. But if we truly care about the civic outcomes of our service-learning practices, there is no other way to get there but to intentionally rearrange our practices with these outcomes fully in mind. In Appendix J on page 82, I provide an exercise for faculty interested in redesigning their service-learning courses to include civic engagement outcomes. I have found this exercise to be useful, not only for individual faculty, but also for departments or programs seeking to move toward greater civic engagement.

References

Alinsky, Saul. 1969. "Native Leadership," in *Reveille for Radicals*. New York: Vintage, 64–75.

Astin, Alexander, et al. 2000. *How Service Learning Affects Students.*
   http://www.gseis.ucla.edu/slc/rhowas.html

Bachman, S.A., with D. Attyah. 2000. "Educating the Artist: A Political Statement," in *The Practice of Change: Concepts and Models for Service-Learning in Women's Studies,* ed. by Barbara J. Balliet and Kerrissa Heffernan. Washington, D.C.: American Association for Higher Education.

Barber, Benjamin R. 1984. *Strong Democracy.* Berkeley, Calif.: University of California Press.

————. 1992. *An Aristocracy of Everyone: The Politics of Education and the Future of America.* New York: Ballantine.

————. 1998. *A Passion for Democracy.* Princeton: Princeton University Press.

————. 1999. "Neither Leaders nor Followers: Citizenship Under Strong Democracy," in *Education for Democracy,* Benjamin Barber & Richard Battistoni, eds. Dubuque, IA: Kendall/Hunt Publishing Company, pp. 164–172.

———— and Richard M. Battistoni. 1993. "A Season of Service: Introducing Service Learning into the Liberal Arts Curriculum." *PS: Political Science & Politics* 26:235–40.

———— and Michael McGrath, eds. 1982. *The Artist and Political Vision.* New Brunswick, NJ: Transaction Books.

Battistoni, Richard M. 1991. "The Civic Education of Future Generations." Baylor Educator (Spring): 6–15.

———. 1995. "Service Learning, Diversity, and the Liberal Arts Curriculum." *Liberal Education,* Volume 81, Number 1 (Winter): pp. 30–35.

———. 1996. "Service-Learning in a Democratic Society: Essential Practices for K-12 Programs." *Community Service-Learning: A Guide to Including Service in the Public School Curriculum.* New York: SUNY Press.

———. 1997a. "Service Learning as Civic Learning: Lessons We Can Learn from Our Students," in *Education for Citizenship: Ideas and Innovations in Political Learning,* ed. Grant Reeher and Joseph Cammarano. New York: Rowman & Littlefield Publishers.

———. 2000. "Democracy, Learning, and Power: Reflections from the Margins of Academic Political Science." Paper presented at the 2000 Annual Meeting of the American Political Science Association, Washington, D.C.

Belenky, Mary Field, Blythe McVicker Clinchy, Nancy Rule Goldberger, and Jill Mattuck Tarule. 1986. *Women's Ways of Knowing: The Development of Self, Voice, and Mind.* New York: Basic Books.

Bellah, Robert, Richard Madsen, William Sullivan, Ann Swidler, and Steven Tipton. 1992. *The Good Society.* New York: Vintage Books.

Bender, Thomas. 1993. *Intellect and Public Life: Essays on the Social History of Academic Intellectuals in the United States.* Baltimore: Johns Hopkins University Press.

Bennett, Stephen Earl. 2000. "Political Apathy and Avoidance of News Media Among Generations X and Y: America's Continuing Problem," in *Education for Civic Engagement in Democracy,* Sheilah Mann & John Patrick, eds. Bloomington, Ind.: ERIC Clearinghouse for Social Studies.

Benson, Lee and Ira Harkavy. 1997. "School and Community in the Global Society," in *Universities and Community Schools.* University of Pennsylvania, Fall-Winter: 16–71

Bloustein, Edward J. 1999. "Community Service: A New Requirement for the Educated Person," in *Education for Democracy,* Benjamin Barber & Richard Battistoni, Eds. Dubuque, Iowa: Kendall/Hunt Publishing Company, pp. 490–493.

Bok, Derek. 1990. *Universities and the Future of America.* Durham, NC: Duke University Press.

Boyer, Ernest. 1994. "Creating the New American College." *The Chronicle of Higher Education.*

————. 1996. "The Scholarship of Engagement," in *The Journal of Public Service and Outreach.* Vol. 1, No. 1, pp. 11–20.

Boyte, Harry. 1989. *Commonwealth: A Return to Citizen Politics.* New York: The Free Press.

————. 1991. "Community Service and Civic Education," in *Phi Beta Kappan* (June).

————. 1999. "Practical Politics," in *Education for Democracy,* Benjamin Barber & Richard Battistoni, eds. Dubuque, Iowa: Kendall/Hunt Publishing Company, pp. 173–9.

————. 2000. "Civic Education as a Craft, Not a Program," in *Education for Civic Engagement in Democracy,* Sheilah Mann & John Patrick, eds. Bloomington, Ind.: ERIC Clearinghouse for Social Studies.

———— and Nancy Kari. 1996. *Building America: The Democratic Promise of Public Work.* Philadelphia: Temple University Press.

————. 2000. "Renewing the Democratic Spirit in American Colleges and Universities: Higher Education as Public Work," in *Civic Responsibility and Higher Education,* Thomas Ehrlich, Ed. Phoenix, AZ: Oryx Press.

Brooks, David. 2001. "The Organization Kid," in *The Atlantic,* Volume 287, Number 4 (April), pp. 40–54.

Burns, James MacGregor. 1979. *Leadership.* New York: Harper & Row, Publishers.

Campbell, David E. 2000. "Social Capital and Service Learning," *PS: Political Science and Politics.* Volume XXXIII, No. 4.

Cammarano, Joseph, Richard Battistoni, & William Hudson. 2000. "Community Service and Citizenship: Is Service-Learning Essential?" Paper presented at the 2000 Annual Meeting of the American Political Science Association, Washington, D.C.

Campus Compact. 1999. *Presidents' Declaration on the Civic Responsibility of Higher Education.* Providence, RI: Campus Compact.

————. 2000. *Benchmarks for Campus/Community Partnerships*. Providence, R.I.: Campus Compact.

Carignan, James. 1998. "Curriculum and Community Connection: The Center for Service Learning at Bates College," in Zlotkowski, Edward, editor, *Successful Service-Learning Programs: New Models of Excellence in Higher Education*. Bolton, Mass.: Anker Publishing Company, Inc.

Carlebach, Stevenson W. and Jefferson A. Singer. 1998. "Applying Service-Learning to the Problem of Prejudice: A Psychology and Theater Course," in *With Service in Mind: Concepts and Models for Service-Learning in Psychology*, ed. by Robert G. Bringle and Donna K. Duffy. Washington, DC: American Association for Higher Education.

Checkoway, Barry. 2001. "Renewing the Civic Mission of the American Research University." *The Journal of Higher Education*. Volume 72, No. 2 (March/April): pp. 127–147.

Chi, Bernadette. 1999. "What's Wrong with This Picture?" *Education for Democracy*, eds. Benjamin R. Barber & Richard M. Battistoni. Des Moines, Iowa: Kendall/Hunt Publishing.

Clark, Todd, Marshall Croddy, William Hayes, & Susan Philips. 1997. "Service Learning as Civic Participation." *Theory into Practice*. Volume 36, Number 3 (Summer).

Clinchy, Blythe McVicker. 1989. "On Critical Thinking and Connected Knowing." *Liberal Education*: 75: 14–19.

Cohen, Jeremy. 2001. "Shouting Fire in a Crowded Classroom: Public Scholarship from Holmes to Homeroom," *Campus Compact Reader*. Vol. 1, Issue 3 (Winter), pp. 11–17.

Coleman, James S. "Social Capital in the Creation of Human Capital." *American Journal of Sociology*. Volume 94 (Supplement): S95–S120.

————. 1990. *Foundations of Social Theory*. Cambridge, MA: Harvard University Press.

Cornell, Drucilla. 1995. *The Imaginary Domain: Abortion, Pornography, and Sexual Harassment*. New York: Routledge.

Cronon, William. 1999. " 'Only Connect': The Goals of a Liberal Education," in *The Key Reporter*. Winter 1999: 2–4.

Cruz, Nadinne. 1998. "Introduction to the Reader: Program Vision and Purpose," *Public Service Research Program Course Reader*. Stanford: Haas Center for Public Service.

Delli Carpini, Michael X., and Scott Keeter. 2000. "What Should Be Learned through Service Learning?" *PS: Political Science and Politics*. Volume XXXIII, No. 4.

————. 1996. *What Americans Know about Politics and Why It Matters*. New Haven: Yale University Press.

de Tocqueville, Alexis. 1945. *Democracy in America*. New York: The Modern Library.

Dewey, John. 1916. *Democracy and Education*. New York: Macmillan Publishing Co.

————. 1938. *Experience and Education*. New York: MacMillan Publishing Co.

Dunlap, Michelle Robin. 2000. *Voices from Community Service and Learning*. Lanham, MD: Bowman & Littlefield.

Etzioni, Amitai. 1993. *The Spirit of Community: Rights, Responsibilities, and the Communitarian Agenda*. New York: Crown Publishers, Inc.

Eyler, Janet and Dwight Giles, Jr. 1999. *Where's the Learning in Service-Learning?* San Francisco: Jossey-Bass Publishers.

Farr, James. "Political Theory," in Experiencing Citizenship: *Concepts and Models for Service-Learning in Political Science*, ed. Richard M. Battistoni and William E. Hudson. Washington, DC: American Association for Higher Education.

Fischer, Robert. 1997. *Let the People Decide: Neighborhood Organizing in America*. Twayne Publishing.

Foos, Cathy Ludlum. 2000. "The Different Voice of Service," in *The Practice of Change: Concepts and Models for Service-Learning in Women's Studies*, Barbara Balliet and Kerrissa Heffernan, eds. Washington, D.C.: American Association for Higher Education.

Freire, Paulo. 1970. *Pedagogy of the Oppressed*. New York: Continuum.

————. 1998. *Pedagogy of Freedom: Ethics, Democracy, and Civic Courage*. Lanham, Md.: Rowman & Littlefield Publishers, Inc.

Gilligan, Carol. 1982. *In a Different Voice: Psychological Theory and Women's Development.* Cambridge, Mass.: Harvard University Press.

Gordon, Rick, Editor. 2000. *Problem Based Service Learning: A Fieldguide for Making a Difference in Higher Education.* Education By Design.

Gray, Maryann J., Elizabeth H. Ondaatje, and Laura Zakaras. 1999. "Combining Service and Learning in Higher Education: Summary Report." Santa Monica, Calif.: Rand Corporation.

Greenleaf, Robert K. 1996. *On Becoming a Servant Leader* (edited by Don M. Frick and Larry C. Spears). San Francisco: Jossey-Bass Publishers.

Guarasci, Richard. 1997. "Community-Based Learning and Intercultural Citizenship," in *Democratic Education in an Age of Difference,* ed. Richard Guarasci and Grant Cornwell. San Francisco: Jossey Bass Publishers.

Harwood Group. 1993. "College Students Talk Politics." Dayton, Ohio: The Kettering Foundation.

Havel, Vaclav. 1997. "New Year's Address to the Nation," in *The Art of the Impossible: Politics as Morality in Practice.* New York: Alfred A. Knopf, 1997.

Heffernan, Kerrissa. 2001. *Fundamentals of Service-Learning Course Construction.* Providence, R.I.: Campus Compact.

Hepburn, Mary A., Richard G. Niemi, and Chris Chapman. 2000. "Service Learning in College Political Science: Queries and Commentary," *PS: Political Science and Politics.* Volume XXXIII, No. 4.

Hildreth, R.W. 2000. "Theorizing Citizenship and Evaluating Public Achievement," *PS: Political Science and Politics.* Volume XXXIII, No. 4.

Hollander, Elizabeth, John Saltmarsh, and Edward Zlotkowski. 2001. "Indicators of Engagement," in Simon, et al. (eds.), *Learning to Serve: Promoting Civil Society Through Service-Learning.*

Hollenbach, David. 1988. *Justice, Peace, and Human Rights: American Catholic Social Ethics in a Pluralistic Context.* New York: Crossroad.

Institute of Politics, Harvard University. 2000. "Attitudes Toward Politics and Public Service." A National Survey of College and University Undergraduates. *HPR online, Harvard Political Review,* Summer 2000. http://www.hpronline.org/survey/.

Jacoby, Russell. 1987. The Last Intellectuals: American Culture in the Age of Academe. New York: Basic Books.

King, Martin Luther, Jr. 1999. "Letter From Birmingham Jail," in *Education for Democracy*, eds. Benjamin R. Barber & Richard M. Battistoni. Des Moines, Iowa: Kendall/Hunt Publishing, pp. 396-404.

Knefelkamp, Lee and Carol Schneider. 1997. "Education for a World Lived in Common with Others," in *Education and Democracy: Re-imagining Liberal Learning*, Robert Orrill, ed. New York: The College Board.

Lakey, Berit, George Lakey, Rod Napier, & Janice M. Robinson. 1995. *Grassroots and Nonprofit Leadership*. New Haven, Conn.: New Society Publishers.

Lappe, Frances Moore and Paul Martin DuBois. 1994. *The Quickening of America: Rebuilding Our Nation, Remaking Our Lives*. San Francisco: Jossey Bass.

Levine, Peter. 2001. "Public Intellectuals and the Influence of Economics," in *Higher Education Exchange*. Dayton, Ohio: The Kettering Foundation.

Lippmann, Walter. 1922. *Public Opinion*. New York: The Free Press.

Liu, Goodwin. "Knowledge, Foundations and Discourse: Philosophical Support for Service-Learning," *Michigan Journal of Community Service-Learning*. Volume 2, pp. 5–18.

Madison, James. 1961. Federalist No. 49, in *The Federalist Papers*. New York: New American Library.

Markus, Gregory, Jeffrey Howard, and David King. 1993. "Integrating Community Service and Classroom Instruction Enhances Learning: Results from an Experiment." *Educational Evaluation and Policy Analysis* 15:4.

Mead, Margaret. 1958. "Thinking Ahead: Why is Education Obsolete?" *Harvard Business Review*, November/December.

Meier, Deborah. 1995. *The Power of Their Ideas*. Boston: Beacon Press.

Mendel-Reyes, Meta. 1995. *Reclaiming Democracy: The Sixties in Politics and Memory*. New York: Routledge.

————. 1997. "Teaching/Theorizing/Practicing Democracy: An Activist's Perspective on Service-Learning in Political Science," in *Experiencing Citizenship: Concepts and Models for Service-Learning in Political Science,* ed. Richard M. Battistoni and William E. Hudson. Washington, D.C.: American Association for Higher Education.

————. 1998. "A Pedagogy for Citizenship: Service Learning and Democratic Education," in *Academic Service Learning: A Pedagogy of Action and Reflection,* Rhoads & Howard, Eds. San Francisco, Calif.: Jossey-Bass Publishers.

Morse, Suzanne. 1990. *Public Leadership Education: Skills for Democratic Citizenship.* Dayton Ohio: The Kettering Foundation.

Morton, Keith. 1997. "Campus and Community at Providence College," in *Expanding Boundaries: Building Civic Responsibility Within Higher Education.* Washington, DC: Corporation for National Service (Volume II, Spring).

————. 1996. "Issues Related to Integrating Service-Learning into the Curriculum," in *Service-Learning in Higher Education: Concepts and Practices,* ed. Barbara Jacoby. San Francisco: Jossey-Bass Publishers.

———— and Rick Battistoni. 1995. "Service and Citizenship: Are They Connected?" *Wingspread Journal* 17.3:17–19 .

National Association of Secretaries of State. 1999. *New Millenium Project—Phase I.* A Nationwide Study of 15–24 Year Old Youth. http://www.nass.org/nass99/youth.htm

National Commission on Civic Renewal. 1998. *A Nation of Spectators: How Civic Disengagement Weakens America and What We Can Do About It.*

National Conference of Catholic Bishops. 1986. *Economic Justice For All.* Washington, D.C.: National Conference of Catholic Bishops.

National Society for Experiential Education. 1990. *Combining Service and Learning: A Resource Book for Community and Public Service.* Raleigh, NC: NSIEE.

Noddings, Nel. 1984. *Caring: A Feminist Approach to Ethics and Moral Education.* Berkeley, University of California Press.

Panetta Institute Poll. 2000. "National Survey of College Students, January 2000." http://www.panettainstitute.org/poll-memo.html.

Phelan, Shane. 1994. Getting Specific. Minneapolis, Minn.: University of Minnesota Press.

Putnam, Robert D. 1993. Making Democracy Work: Civic Traditions in Modern Italy (with Robert Leonardi and Raffaella Y. Nanetti). Princeton: Princeton University Press.

————. 1995. "Bowling Alone: America's Declining Social Capital." *Journal of Democracy* Volume 6:1:65–78.

————. 2000. *Bowling Alone: The Collapse and Revival of American Community.* New York: Simon & Schuster.

Rawls, John. 1971. *A Theory of Justice.* Cambridge, MA: Harvard University Press.

Reagon, Bernice Johnson. 1998. "Coalition Politics: Turning the Century," in *Race, Class and Gender: An Anthology* (3d ed.), Anderson & Collins, eds., pp. 517–523.

Reardon, Kenneth. 1997. "Institutionalizing Community Service Learning at Major Research University: The Case of the East St. Louis Action Research Project," *Michigan Journal of Community Service Learning.* Volume 4.

Rimmerman, Craig. 1997. *The New Citizenship: Unconventional Politics, Activism, and Service.* Boulder, Colo.: Westview Press.

————. 1997a. "Teaching American Politics through Service: Reflections on a Pedagogical Strategy," in *Education for Citizenship: Ideas and Innovations in Political Learning,* ed. Grant Reeher and Joseph Cammarano. New York: Rowman & Littlefield Publishers, Inc.

Rogers, Mary Beth. 1990. *Cold Anger: A Story of Faith and Power Politics.* University of North Texas Press.

Saltmarsh, John and Elizabeth Hollander. 2000. "Off the Playground of Higher Education." *PEGS Journal* (Spring, forthcoming).

Sax, L.J., A.W. Astin, W.S. Korn, and K.M. Mahoney. 1999, 2000. "The American Freshman: National Norms for Fall 1999 & 2000." Los Angeles, Calif.: Higher Education Research Institute.

Sax, Linda J. and Alexander W. Astin. 1997. "The Benefits of Service: Evidence From Undergraduates, *Educational Record.* Volume 78: pp. 25–32.

Schneider, Carol Geary. 2001. "Toward the Engaged Academy: New Scholarship, New Teaching," *Liberal Education,* Volume 87, Number 1 (Winter).

Stanton, Timothy. 1992. 'Response,' in "Education for Democracy: Challenges and Prospects," in *The Civic Arts Review.* Volume 5, Number 4, Fall 1992.

Sullivan, William M. 1995. *Work and Integrity: The Crisis and Promise of Professionalism in America.* New York: HarperCollins Publishers.

Swezey, Erin D. 1990. "Grounded in Justice: Service Learning from a Faith Perspective," in *Community Service as Values Education,* Delve, Mintz, & Stewart, eds. San Francisco: Jossey-Bass Publishers.

Tarrance Group and Lake, Snell, Perry & Associates. 1999. "New Millennium Project—Phase 1: A Nationwide Study of 15–25 Year Old Youth." Washington, D.C.: National Association of Secretaries of State.

Tocqueville, Alexis de. 1945 [1835]. *Democracy in America.* New York: The Modern Library.

Tronto, Joan. 1993. *Moral Boundaries: A Political Argument for an Ethic of Care.* New York: Routledge.

Wade, Rahima, ed. 1997. *Community Service Learning: A Guide to Including Service in the Public School Curriculum.* Albany: State University of New York Press.

Walker, Tobi. 2000. "The Service/Politics Split: Rethinking Service to Teach Political Engagement," *PS: Political Science and Politics.* Volume XXXIII, No. 4.

—————. 2000a. "Service and Politics: The Lost Connection." An unpublished paper prepared for The Ford Foundation. May 30.

Walt Whitman Center. 1996. *Measuring Citizenship: Assessing the Impact of Service Learning on America's Youth.* New Brunswick: Walt Whitman Center, Rutgers University.

Westheimer, Joel, and Joseph Kahne. 2000. "Service Learning Required." *Education Week,* January 26. http://www.educationweek.org/ew/ew

Whitman, Walt. 1999. "Democratic Vistas," in *Education for Democracy,* Benjamin Barber & Richard Battistoni, Eds. Dubuque, Iowa: Kendall/Hunt Publishing Company, pp. 47–54.

Wingspread Group on Higher Education. 1993. *An American Imperative: Higher Expectations for Higher Education.* Racine, Wisconsin: The Johnson Foundation.

Young, Iris Marion. 1997. *Intersecting Voices: Dilemmas of Gender, Political Philosophy, and Policy.* Princeton, N.J.: Princeton University Press.

————. 1990. *Justice and the Politics of Difference.* Princeton, N.J.: Princeton University Press.

Appendix

This appendix contains resources for moving students from service to civic engagement, and includes sample course assignments, exercises, and reflection questions.

Appendix A

HOW DO YOU DEFINE CITIZENSHIP?

People define citizenship in many different ways. Represented below are some examples of what people would call "good citizenship." Place a "1" next to the action that most closely models your own idea of good citizenship. Place a "2" next to the action that is the second closest, etc., up to 15.

_____ Joining the armed forces.

_____ Helping to start an after-school program for children whose parents work.

_____ Talking with a friend about a social issue of importance to you.

_____ Working for a candidate in a local election.

_____ Walking a frail person across a busy street.

_____ Picketing and protesting at a local plant that has laid off a large number of its workforce.

_____ Giving $50 to the United Way.

_____ Leaving your car at home and biking or walking to work/school every day.

_____ Tutoring a migrant worker.

_____ Adopting an eight-year old boy.

_____ Providing dinner once a week at a homeless shelter.

_____ Visiting different houses of worship (churches, synagogues, mosques, etc.) every week to learn about different religions in the community.

_____ Giving blood.

_____ Working as a state legislator.

_____ Voting.

Adapted from Nadinne Cruz, "How Do You Define Service?" (February, 1996)

Appendix B
REFLECTION QUESTIONS THAT TAP CIVIC DIMENSIONS

What is citizenship? What does it mean to be a citizen in a democracy? As a student at [Providence College], you are both a resident of the [city of Providence] and of the United States. But do you consider yourself to be a "citizen" of both/either? What have you done—concretely—in the past year to exercise your rights and fulfill your civic responsibilities, in the [City of Providence], and in the U.S.?

What is democracy? Can you describe a community to which you belong that you would define as democratic? Is the organization within which you serve democratic? Does it matter?

What is the civic role of your chosen profession/discipline? What are the public/civic dimensions of your anticipated work? What expectations does a democratic community place upon you as an individual? Upon you in your professional capacity?

What is your agency's/school's/CBO's mission, governance structure, funding base? In what ways is the organization with which you work connected with government, foundation, and corporate policies and regulations?

Much of the discussion around "diversity," "community," and "service" centers around questions of power, privilege, and access in the public sphere. Can you think—concretely and specifically—about times and places where you've felt privileged and included, or alternatively marginalized and excluded, based on characteristics related to your "identity" (e.g., race, ethnicity, "culture," language, religion, age, economic class, gender, sexual orientation, ability/disability, appearance, opinions/ideas)? Think about the people you are in relationship with at your service site. What do you think causes them to matter or be marginalized in mainstream American communities and culture? How do the categories that have affected you—positively or negatively—affect them? How do you think they perceive you and your identity?

Take a public policy issue of concern to you. How does it relate to your community service placement? Is the agency/school within which you work/serve organized to address this public policy issue? How?

To what degree do you see yourself as responsive to the concerns of the community? To what degree do you see your college/university as responsive to the concerns of the community? To what degree do you see your fellow students as responsive to the concerns of the community? To what degree do you see the organization or agency where you serve as responsive to the concerns of the community?

Appendix C

PUBLIC PROBLEM STATEMENT AND
ORGANIZATIONAL ISSUE RESEARCH

Many if not all of the organizations or programs that you work with were developed self-consciously in response to a "public problem." You may have learned about this through your investigation of the organizations' or programs' history.

A good problem statement does the following:

- Concisely states a situation that needs to be changed
- States who/what is affected
- Quantifies the problem
- Addresses a public issue related to the organizational needs/purposes

Write a public problem statement for your organization. Consider the following:

Causes

- Why does the problem exist?
- What makes it a "public" problem?
- Is there more than one cause?
- Are the causes interdependent?

Consequences

- What are the consequences of the problem?
- How many people does it affect?
- Are there political, cultural, & economic effects?

Methodology

Describe how you went about gathering the information used to establish your problem statement.

- What were your sources (reports, interviews, internet, newspapers, etc.)?
- How were members of your organization or community involved in developing the statement?
- How broadly is this recognized as a public problem?
- How does the organization frame the reasons for the existence of the problem?
- How does the organization frame the problem as a public problem?
- How does the organization frame the causes of the problem?
- How does the organization frame the consequences of the problem?

After writing your brief problem statement, write a 5- to 7-page paper describing the "public problem" in depth. Conduct a literature survey and include what the literature suggests about causes and consequences of the problem. While the problem statement may define the problem in somewhat generic terms, your paper should detail the local realities of the public problem, and include how local developments, laws, and social conditions impact how the problem is locally manifested.

Taken from PSP 401: Community Service Practicum (Fall 1999)
Rick Battistoni & Dana Farrell, Instructors
Providence College

Appendix D
PHILOSOPHY OF SERVICE ASSIGNMENT

In your first paper, you were asked to construct your own story of service. This last assignment asks you to take this one step further, to articulate your "philosophy of service." As discussed in class, in its final form this will be a one-paragraph statement of your philosophy of service followed by a narrative explaining the paragraph statement. Since this assignment is the final one for the course, among the things you might want to consider are: your definition of service; what values, motivations, or goals underlay your understanding of service and the service you choose/want to do; the relationship you seek to establish with those whom you serve (including how you understand the people being served, their "needs," how you prepare for entering and exiting service, etc.); how you understand "community" and how that impacts your philosophy of service; how—if at all—issues of citizenship and/or politics enter into your philosophy of service. In the narrative portion of the paper, you might also want to identify readings or class discussions that were "transformative" in your thinking about service and/or the development of this statement.

Remember, you are to bring a draft of your paragraph-long philosophy of service for comments and questions by the rest of the class, on Thursday, November 30. Your final version, with narrative accompaniment, is due by Thursday, December 14 (the day scheduled for our final exam).

Taken from PSP 101: Introduction to Service in Democratic Communities (Fall 2000)
Rick Battistoni, Instructor
Providence College

Appendix E
SEMESTER PROJECT: DRAMA AND PUBLIC VALUE

The purpose of the semester project is to give you a chance to use your growing knowledge of drama to help produce something of public value: a drama class, a performance, a piece of research someone can use to improve a drama-related undertaking. By producing something of more than formal, classroom value, you can strengthen your ownership of new concepts and techniques while at the same time sharing your knowledge with others in the surrounding community. You have two options:

Option A: A 3,000-word "research" paper on a topic requested by a drama-related group. For example, a school drama program might want to know about the kinds of resources available to such a program. A community theater may want to know more about a particular kind of drama it is thinking of performing, or about dramatic works on a certain theme. Still another group may want help in actually writing a play or the audience notes to accompany a performance. It is up to you to find a research "sponsor." However, Jennifer Webster at the Bentley Service-Learning Center can give you a hand. In the event that you and she cannot find a sponsor, I will serve as the sponsor of last resort.

Option B: A minimum of 20 hours of in-person participation in a school drama program, community theater or nonprofit theater production plus three 3-part journal entries (see journal instructions). This option is for individuals who would rather spend their time "on site" than "behind the scenes." NOTE: Your work must involve you in drama-related activities. You may NOT work on the business side. See the attached list for service options identified by Jennifer Webster at the Bentley Service-Learning Center.

Taken from Forms of Drama (Spring 2001)
Edward Zlotkowski, Instructor
Bentley College

Appendix F
ACTION PLANS ASSIGNMENT

The final requirement of this course is the development and presentation of a public advocacy campaign, which should integrate your public policy research, your community service experience, and an understanding of making policy change.

What is a public advocacy campaign? An advocacy campaign should:

1. educate citizens about an issue;

2. inspire them to try to make change;

3. provide tools for that effort.

Components of the public advocacy campaign could include:

- A letter writing campaign developed around a specific piece of legislation.

- A citizen lobbying effort.

- A protest, boycott, or rally.

- A public service ad campaign.

The key to an effective campaign is creativity. Ask yourself: How can the campaign inspire people to move beyond their apathy to ACTION?

Your action plan should be based on your policy research and your community service experience. Identify a need, policy, or perspective that needs to be addressed, and then figure out a way to address it. For example, if you have been working at a soup kitchen and you did your research on state plans to alter food stamp regulations, your advocacy campaign should focus on those issues.

Remember: Your audience is not the clients of a social service agency. In other words, do not develop a plan that involves training volunteers to assist clients in filling out food stamp applicants. Rather, your advocacy campaign might focus on policy change, helping to create or support a piece of legislation, getting food kitchen clients onto a community board, or organizing a petition to encourage the development commission to improve grocery store access.

The Ground Rules

You will make an oral presentation to the class; any supplemental visual or written materials will be submitted to your instructors. Your grade will be determined primarily by your oral presentation.

Imagine the class is an organization that has decided to work on the issue you have selected. Your job is to develop a comprehensive action plan for the group to undertake. You have 10 minutes to present the plan to the group. Cover all the major aspects of the plan:

- Briefly summarize the focus or goal of your advocacy. Your issue should be broad and visionary— for example, ending domestic violence—but you should not spend much time explaining why you chose that issue. Instead, your focus should be limited in scope and result in clear outcomes. For example: "Our goal is to ensure bi-partisan support for Assembly Bill 220, which will increase funding for domestic violence shelters in New Jersey."

- Present the components of your plan as thoroughly as possible. If there is a letter writing campaign, prepare draft letters. If your organization's members will be lobbying, prepare lobbying points for a fact sheet. If you are planning a media campaign, prepare draft press releases and develop press events. If you will be seeking support from others in the community, explain how you will target others and provide a sample of your public education strategies. Be creative in your methods and techniques.

Some questions to consider:

- Who are the key players—policy makers, opinion leaders, and organization directors—that you need to affect?

- Are there organizations that should join your coalition? What are the advantages to a coalition? What are the disadvantages? How will you persuade them to work with you? What will be the impact if you don't ask them to join?

- What is your strategy (e.g.: letter writing campaign, rally, protest)?

- What kind of advocacy will you be pursuing: public, administrative, or legislative? (See Amidiei page 6 for an explanation of those terms.)

- Why have you chosen this strategy? Be specific and persuasive.

As you think about your action plan, be sure to review *So You Want to Make Difference: Advocacy is the Key* for ideas and methods.

Taken from Political Science 440: Becoming a Public Citizen (Fall 1995)
Tobi Walker and Ruth B. Mandel
Rutgers, the State University of New Jersey

Appendix G
COALITION BUILDING EXERCISE

The purpose of this exercise is to simulate, through a role-playing activity, the process of defining one's interests and/or stake in an issue and moving from there to identify natural "allies" and build coalitions around the issue.

Step 1:   Identify a "public issue" of concern on your campus.

Step 2:   Brainstorm together the individuals, offices, or student groups on campus that would need to be at the table in any resolution of the identified issue. When consensus is reached about a particular "stakeholder," write the name of the individual/office/group down on an index card. (The number of stakeholders identified should be equal to the number of participants involved in this exercise).

Step 3:   Hand out one of the cards to each participant. Each stakeholder should take a few minutes to formulate that individual's or group's beginning response to the issue in question. After giving time to formulate your basic "line" or arguments, begin circulating, and without identifying who you are, share with other stakeholders your own position(s) and listen to those of other participants playing their own stakeholder roles.

Step 4:   Figure out which participants would likely be allied with you based on what you hear from each, and which would likely be opponents or challenges in building a coalition to get the issue addressed in ways that closely align with your own interest. Group together according to coalitions.

Step 5:   Come together as an entire group and allow each participant to share their position and who they see themselves allied with. Try to guess which individual/group each participant has represented in this simulated exercise.

Debriefing/Reflection Questions

- What did you learn from this simulation about coalition building?

- What was the most difficult challenge for you in deciding which coalitions to form?

- Who was your "most surprising ally," from your perspective?

- How might such an exercise work with a public issue that affects the organization you serve?

Appendix H
ORGANIZATIONAL ACTION RESEARCH ASSIGNMENT

This introductory assignment is designed for you to learn about the mission, history, staffing, governance, and budget of the community-based organization where you are working. You are not limited to gathering information from the primary contact person at the organization. Try to get as broad and as comprehensive a view of the organization as possible, which means that the more people you talk to, the better off you'll be! In addition to answering the questions below, please submit as much organizational literature as you can collect, including public relations material, application forms, pamphlets, etc.

Name of Organization/School:

- Brief History and Founders

- Mission Statement

- Summary of vision: What would this organization like to accomplish/become? What are they trying to make happen?

- How did the vision of the organization evolve? What are the key points of development?

- Who were the founders? What roles did they initially play in the organization? Were they, themselves, educators, community activists, organizers? Are the founders still involved?

- Describe the population that the organization serves.

- What geographic area does the organization serve? Are there boundaries?

- Given what you've learned about the organization, what are the three most important areas of need around which student service opportunities can be designed?

- Budget: How much is it and from what sources? What can you infer about the budget in terms of the organization's priorities? How do you see the budget relating to the organization's mission? (Please attach a copy of the annual budget).

- By whom are the financial records kept?

- What grant seeking has occurred? From what sources and with what success? Has the organization attempted any other kinds of fundraising (e.g., special events, personal solicitation, direct mail)?

- How many paid staff are employed by the organization? What are their roles?

- Would you characterized the staff as having a hierarchical or nonhierarchical structure? (Please attach a graphic representation of the organizational chart/staff structure.)

- Is there a board of directors? If so, who are the board members? How were they recruited? What skills do they bring to the organization? How often does the board meet? What are the most important challenges facing the board? What are the most important accomplishments of the board?

- How will the information that you learned from completing this assignment increase your effectiveness in your service work with this organization?

- From whom (or what) did you learn the information necessary to complete this assignment?

Taken from PSP 401: Community Service Practicum (Fall 1999)
Rick Battistoni & Dana Farrell, Instructors
Providence College

Appendix I

FINAL SERVICE SITE TEAM
PRESENTATION ASSIGNMENT

In the Fall, 2000, I experimented with having students at different kinds of community service sites read different materials, related to the issues they were dealing with in their service work. For a final project, students were asked to draw upon their specific service experiences to arrive at some conclusions about the "big picture issues" involved in their work over the course of the semester. I gave each team of students the following set of assignment parameters.

If you look at the syllabus for this course, it says that "30 percent of your final grade will be based on your contribution to two service-site team presentations, and your work on a final project connected to your service and related readings…" You have already done one site team presentation; the second—to be done the last week of class—is meant to allow you to move beyond your community service work to examine the "bigger picture" issues involved, with the resource of outside readings to assist you. I provide some parameters for each of these presentations below. The "final project"—due by December 14, should flow out of the final site presentations. We can talk about these in class.

School Sites

Your presentation should take off from the starting point of your service this semester to look at the larger educational issues/problems that your service is attempting to address. How would you define these issues, based on your experiences this semester? In *The Power of Their Ideas,* Deborah Meier makes a number of arguments about education and schools based on her experiences with Central Park East. What are her main arguments? Do you think they are applicable to your school? Why or why not? Is her vision for education something that would enhance the learning of children that you work with? For the St. Patrick's School group, do her arguments, which are largely about public education, apply to a private school like the one you're serving in?

Sunrise House

Your presentation should take off from the starting point of your service this semester to look at the larger issues of HIV/AIDS and/or public health. Based on your experience, how would you define the larger issues that underlie the problems your service addresses? The McKinlay essay, though concerned with illness and health care more generally, presents the metaphor of working "downstream" vs. "upstream." Is your service at Sunrise a "downstream endeavor," as McKinlay defines it. What would it mean to focus upstream? And what issues are posed by the Sullivan and Fuller essays for anyone in your position attempting to focus upstream on the problem of HIV/AIDS?

Southside Community Land Trust

Your presentation should take off from the starting point of your service this semester to look at the larger issues of urban/community gardens, community-supported agriculture, and community development. Based on your experience, how have you come to define these larger issues? The Seedfolks book and the excerpts from *Sharing the Harvest* provide a context for examining these issues. What is community-supported agriculture, and how does it tie in with your work at Southside? How does the work you're doing contribute to community development, especially with respect to creating community within a diverse population?

Taken from PSP 101: Introduction to Service in Democratic Communities (Fall 2000)
Rick Battistoni, Instructor
Providence College

Appendix J
CURRICULAR REVISION EXERCISE*

Choose an academic department at your institution (preferably your own), to begin thinking about moving that department toward "civic engagement."

1. List courses in this department (along with the faculty who teach them) that you think would be critical building blocks for civic engagement.

2. Now, choose one of these listed courses (preferably one you teach or have taught in the past), and modify it to include a civic engagement dimension.

3. Overall goals for the course:

4. What you would like a civic engagement component to contribute to achieving those goals (i.e., concepts, skills, etc.)?

5. Ways of looking at civic engagement that tie in with the course content (e.g., connections to disciplinary perspectives, public problems, professional ethics):

6. Kinds of community projects, placements, or research that would be appropriate to achieving the civic outcomes for the course:

7. Adjustments you might want/need to make to course requirements (readings, writing assignments, etc.) to accommodate and integrate the civic engagement component of the course:

8. Your primary strategy to help students reflect on the civic dimensions of the course, including the community-based component:

*Adapted from Edward Zlotkowski, "Course Revision Exercise," 1998.

Appendix K
RHETORIC AND PUBLIC OPINION PAPER ASSIGNMENT

For this paper, you will need to understand how the organization you are working with understands and uses public opinion. As we have noted, the organization you are working with developed in response to a "public problem," and sees itself as serving particular "publics." As such, the organization has (or should have) a sense of how this problem is viewed by the public, how the public responds to the problem, and of strategies for using or swaying public opinion concerning the image of the organization and the problem it addresses.

For this paper, you are to indicate how your organization garners public opinion and how this information is used to further the organization's mission. You also are to evaluate the organization's definition and use of public opinion. In doing so, consider the following questions.

- Does the organization have institutionalized means for gathering public opinion about the organization and the problem(s) it addresses? If so, what are they? What are the strengths and weaknesses of these means?

- Does the organization use public opinion to achieve its mission? If so, how? How does the organization's perception of public opinion influence the public messages of the organization?

- Does the organization try to change public opinion to achieve its mission? If so, how is this indicated in the organization's public messages?

- How do organizational members articulate their perceptions of public understandings of the organization and problem(s) it addresses? In other words, do their understandings of public opinions of the organization come from sources other than institutionalized means? How do organizational members talk about what "the public" thinks concerning the organization and its mission?

- Suppose the organization's executive director hired you to evaluate how they gather and use public opinion. What recommendations would you make to improve organizational members' understandings and use of public opinion?

Your paper should be 3 to 5 pages, typed, double-spaced.

Taken from Comm 4300: Rhetoric and Civic Community
Gerard A. Hauser and Christy Standerfer, Instructors
University of Colorado, Boulder